D1636513

CCCC Studies in Writing & Rhetoric

THE COMMUNITY COLLEGE WRITER

The Community College Writer

Exceeding Expectations

Howard Tinberg and Jean-Paul Nadeau

A Study Funded by the Calderwood Writing
Initiative and Bristol Community College

Southern Illinois University Press
Carbondale and Edwardsville

Copyright © 2010 by the Conference on College Composition and Communication of the National Council of Teachers of English
All rights reserved
Printed in the United States of America

13   12   11   10   4   3   2   1

Publication partially funded by a subvention grant from the Conference on College Composition and Communication of the National Council of Teachers of English.

Library of Congress Cataloging-in-Publication Data
Tinberg, Howard B., 1953–
  The community college writer : exceeding expectations / Howard Tinberg and Jean-Paul Nadeau.
      p. cm. — (CCCC studies in writing & rhetoric)
  "A study funded by the Calderwood Writing Initiative and Bristol Community College."
  Includes bibliographical references and index.
  ISBN-13: 978-0-8093-2956-4 (alk. paper)
  ISBN-10: 0-8093-2956-5 (alk. paper)
  eISBN: 0-8093-8577-5
  1. English language—Rhetoric—Study and teaching—United States. 2. English language—Composition and exercises—Study and teaching—United States. I. Nadeau, Jean-Paul, 1968– II. Conference on College Composition and Communication (U.S.). III. Title.
  PE1405.U6T56 2010
  808'.0420711—dc22   2009021454

Printed on recycled paper. ♻

The paper used in this publication meets the minimum requirements of American National Standard for Information Sciences—Permanence of Paper for Printed Library Materials, ANSI z39.48-1992. ∞

CONTENTS

ACKNOWLEDGMENTS

We wish to thank the students who participated in this study, particularly those presented in the cases. Given all that they were sorting out during their first semester at college, it was brave of them to participate in a project that would primarily benefit other students. We are thankful that they felt comfortable enough with us to share their struggles, whether with writing, college, or life in general, as well as their successes (one student burst into our offices to share, excitedly, that she had earned an A on her last math exam).

We are grateful as well to colleagues Jody Millward, Kip Strasma, and Jeff Klausman, who graciously agreed to survey a significant group of new students at Santa Barbara City College, Illinois Central College, and Whatcom Community College (Bellingham, Washington), respectively. Their efforts allowed us to place our findings within a national context. We also want to acknowledge faculty participants at our own college. Given the demands on full- and part-time faculty, we are extremely grateful for the many who donated their valuable time to help this project move forward. Of special note are those who sat with us for an interview: Elizabeth Alcock, Phoebe Blackburn, Joanna Duponte, Danielle Finch, Michael Geary, Kevin Garganta, Dennis Grieco, Kathy Lund, Marcia McKee, Marisa Millard, and Jim Warner.

We couldn't have conducted such a study in the first place without the support of the Calderwood Foundation, whose executive director, John Brereton, provided sustained support throughout the project. Nancy Sommers, who served as our consultant, and John gave up much of their time to offer timely and instrumental feedback.

Thanks must also go to administrators at Bristol who worked with us throughout the grant process. Vice President Rhonda Gabovitz and her assistant Raynette Demello helped us select a randomized, representative cohort and sort through mounds of data. Dean Joanne Preston continually offered her assistance to the project. Associate Vice President Karen Dixon helped shepherd our project through the budget-building stage.

Finally, we can't give enough praise and thanks to our technical assistant Lynne Bernier, who contributed much more than data entry and statistical calculations (though the work there was indeed tremendous). Lynne shared her keen insights in the realm of study design and her understanding of college students. Without her, it would have been much more difficult to retain students in the study. From mailings, phone calls, and e-mails to working with statistical software, copying student papers, and compiling portfolios, Lynne did everything she could to assist with this research. Lynne, thank you.

THE COMMUNITY COLLEGE WRITER

1

Introduction and Rationale

AS FACULTY WITH A combined three decades of experience teaching first-year college composition, we recognize the importance of what Nick Tingle has called the "transitional space." First-year composition is so often a crash course in navigating the twists and turns of the "academic terrain," as Tingle puts it (4). Within the context of community colleges, the first-semester writing course is especially crucial, given the varied levels of student preparedness and the extent of work and family demands. So many students fail to persist when confronting this very demanding first semester of college.

To what extent does writing instruction play a part in acclimating students in that first semester or, indeed, in placing a formidable obstacle before them? Certainly, we'd been asking that question for a long time as we continued to revise our own composition pedagogy and as we, alas, witnessed students struggle to meet the demands not only of our own courses but of the many challenging subjects in their first year of college. But did we really have a handle on the specific nature of the writing challenges for these novice college students?

Both of us, fortunately, came to this study with extensive work in multidisciplinary writing centers and thus have a keen appreciation of the varied writing demands placed on college students, especially community college students. But we felt the need to research in a systematic way the nature and extent of those demands. What kinds of writing were being assigned both in the English composition classroom and the many subjects that first-semester students typically took? As community college faculty, we were intrigued by the speculation that in some way the rhetorical challenges placed before these novice writers might reflect a tilt toward the career-based literacies, given the significant attention paid to career training at the college. Would students and faculty alike resist the conventional modes of academic writing in favor of assignments that explicitly prepare students for the workplace? Our research indicated otherwise: true to the college's comprehensive mission to promote both workplace and academic literacies, faculty assignments aimed to promote what Russel Durst has called "reflective instrumentalism," written forms that attempt to bridge the gap between writing for work and writing for the classroom (170). Perhaps not surprisingly, courses outside English were those most likely to engage students in such thoughtfully pragmatic work.

What role does writing have in engaging students? Does writing, as Richard Light's study suggests, have a significant role in connecting undergraduates to their classroom experiences (55)? Conversely, does writing pose certain obstacles for students, especially those students unprepared to write for a variety of audiences and in a variety of forms? While first-semester composition aims to give students some sense of rhetorical knowledge (modeling questions such as, Whom am I writing for? What is my purpose in writing?), some have argued that the courses coming after this initial experience provide a deeper understanding of the writing process, deeper because the writing is embedded in the conventions of disciplines and employs the concepts and terms essential to probing complex issues. Students' analytical skills are thus concurrently enhanced by their exposure to increasingly varied and detailed information. "Writers need concepts and knowledge to think with," writes Lee Ann Carroll, concepts and knowledge drawn from the disciplines (116). We intend to discover how our students think through the writing they do in their first semester at college.

WHAT WE WANTED TO KNOW

While our experience working as tutors in a multidisciplinary writing lab offered a glimpse of writing instruction beyond the first year required course in composition, we realized that a systematic study needed to be done of that instruction. Of course, we also wanted to know the expectations, experience, understanding, and practices that first-semester students brought to their college work. Would they, for example, have had prior experience revising their writing, guided by feedback either from peers or teachers? Indeed, would they have had experience writing extensively in subjects other than English or language arts? In other words, to what extent did faculty expectations match those of first-semester students? Core questions needed to be addressed, the foremost being

1. How much writing was assigned beyond the required basic and college-level writing courses? Were students prepared for the volume of writing required?
2. To what extent were students writing in genres other than the essay? Did students expect to write in modes other than the academic essay?
3. What role did revision have in writing instruction at the college? How did students' understanding of this task differ from that of faculty?
4. When faculty assessed student writing, was the emphasis on higher- or lower-order concerns? Did faculty feedback match student expectations?
5. How extensive was faculty commentary on student writing? What purpose did that commentary serve? To explain a grade? To guide revision? Both? How did students process the commentary?

While our study focuses on students and faculty at the community college, we recognize the importance of these questions for all who have a stake in college writing instruction, at both four- and two-year institutions. It is our hope that others may see the virtue—indeed, the necessity—of investigating the challenges facing writers new to college and their responses to those challenges.

POSITIONING OURSELVES

"All researchers are positioned," writes Elizabeth Chiseri-Strater, "whether they write about it explicitly, or not at all" (115). Chiseri-

Strater refers here to researchers across disciplines and to all studies, whether qualitative or quantitative: the relationship between the researcher and the subject researched invariably affects the outcome of the study. Our study is no different. Who we are, who shaped us professionally, how we came to teach at the community college: all these matters we will share from the outset, especially as they affect the shaping of data. We make no claim to absolute objectivity. Indeed, over the time that we have worked with our cohort of students, we have come to know them more fully than we would as classroom instructors. For some, we served as mentors, advisors, tutors.

Howard Tinberg's Narrative

Since both of us have worked in writing centers—as tutors and as directors—it seemed natural to offer our tutoring services to students participating in the project. Over the decade and a half that I've directed and tutored in our college's center, I've found the opportunity to work with writers one-on-one to be one of the most rewarding aspects of my professional life. I've enjoyed being able to focus on the work of a single student and to engage in meaningful conversation with students about their work. And when I've had the opportunity to work with a student over several visits, I was fortunate enough to develop a working relationship with that student and to draw from my knowledge to gauge the writer's development. At the community college, those students are likely to be older than a traditionally aged college student, often the first in the family to go to college, likely working at least part-time off campus, and with a family of their own—factors that invariably produce heightened motivation, if, at times, increased demands on their time.

Like so many of my students, my three siblings and I were the first generation in our family to go to college. And, again like so many of these students, we had little in the way of academic support at home since our parents, refugees from the European Holocaust (where they had lost everyone on both sides of the family), had no formal education and knew no English when they arrived but knew several other languages, including German, Russian, Polish, and Yiddish. We were working class, poorer than I had realized, insulated as I was by parents who worked hard and saved as much as they possibly could. My father worked as a tailor, first in a department store—at minimum wage and paid by the piece. We lived for a time in Portland, Oregon, but moved south to Los Angeles—in part to restore my father to health, who, unknown to me and my siblings at the time, was dying of pancreatic cancer. Where but in paradise might a struggling tailor find health and economic happiness? Indeed, my father would eventually open up two tailoring shops, one in Hollywood where, to our astonishment, he began to count screen actors as his customers ("The Tailor to the Stars," we'd later remark). Many years later, when reading Mike Rose's memoir *Lives on the Boundary,* a book that moved me in a profoundly personal way, I came across Rose's description of a similar journey, one that resonated deeply with me: "My father had moved to California with faint hopes about health and a belief in his child's future, drawn by that far edge of America where the sun descends into green water. What he found was a city that was warm, verdant, vast, and indifferent as a starlet in a sports bar. Altoona receded quickly, and my parents must have felt isolated and deceived. They had fallen into an abyss of paradise—two more settlers trying to make a go of it in the City of the Angels" (13).

Here they were, my parents, true orphans after the war, trying desperately to build from the ashes—perhaps drawn, as Rose's father had been, by what educator Lee Shulman, another immigrant's kid, has called "visions of the possible" (212). At this distance, now many decades removed from my youth, I cannot pretend to speak for my parents' hopes and dreams: they were in some ways mysterious even to us, their children. But this much I can say: each of us inherited a tenacious determination to succeed, no doubt buttressed by an equally tenacious fear of failure. When I see so many of my students at our community college working full time, taking a full-time course load, and expressing a determination to succeed at all costs even as they are bearing the burdens of past failures, I catch a glimmer of myself long ago. I do not grimace when my students tell me that they enrolled at our college to find a well-paying job rather than out of a desire to learn for learning's sake. My mother had to work as a school cafeteria worker after the death of my father because our family was stretched financially, so I can sympathize with my students' aims. But I should add this: while my parents did not have formal education, all of my siblings were raised to grant education an intrinsic value, although my eldest brother, I am told, had to fight for the right to attend college rather than go out to "work." I surmise, after the fact, that our religious upbringing—as observant Jews, we followed Biblical dietary laws, attended Hebrew school, received bar/bat mitzvahs—had much to do with giving us a respect "for the book," for reading, and for the life of the mind. Who should be surprised, then, that each of us has a doctorate degree?

I arrived at our public community college with a PhD in British Romantic literature, having recently taught at a private university. I was still new to the field of composition and rhetoric and had not taught full-time at a community college. I had much to learn on both counts. From the vantage point of two decades later, I realize now that culture shock was unavoidable. Despite my own working-class background, I stood committed to the liberal arts, most especially to the transformative power of literature. Inevitably, that commitment clashed with the comprehensive and, as some have noted, contradictory mission of the community college to prepare students both for transfer to a baccalaureate institution and for the workplace. A creeping vocationalism at community colleges has been well documented:

> When they first appeared at the turn of the [twentieth] century, community colleges were largely liberal-arts-oriented institutions, providing many students with the first leg of their baccalaureate preparation and others with a terminal general education. But over the years, this orientation changed radically. Community colleges added programs in adult education, community education, remedial education, and most importantly occupational education. Today, vocational education is the dominant program in the community college, enrolling between 40 and 60% (depending on the estimate) of community college students. . . . (Dougherty 191)

At my college, the increasing vocationalism has been most apparent in the proliferating number of certificate programs awarded for those interested in upgrading their job skills. But I see this enhanced vocationalism in the expectations of students and colleagues alike—hardly unique to the community college, as Durst has shown, but no doubt heightened by the difficult challenges faced by our students (51). Students expect to receive skills that they can market and apply in their careers. As I noted above, I can hardly diminish this reasonable ambition. I have over the years altered my approach to teaching (especially in composition) to accommodate the growing utilitarian culture of the college. Rather than focus on the writing of essays exclusively, I have my students write in a variety of genres: memoir, review, annotation, trend analysis, brochure, and journal web log (blog) as well as essay. Reading in my composition classes is limited to samples of genres, often done for popular magazines and Web sites. In contrast, when I arrived at the college, I had students read and write about strictly academic texts—drawn from David Bartholomae and Anthony Petrosky's *Ways of Reading*. Taking my cue from the editors of that textbook, I encouraged the notion that reading difficult texts can be good for you. I saw quickly that no matter how hard I tried I could not get students to inhabit these texts. Reading challenging texts remains a problem for students in my British literature courses, which are typically underenrolled. My philosophy in those courses is to try to do more with fewer readings and to create thematic and historical connections among the readings. Drawing from process-centered approaches to composition, I've also attempted to place student writing at the center of my literature survey courses: through weekly reader response journals, which we share at the end of each week, and invitations to create imagined scenarios (composing a new ending for a novel or play, for example, or a Web-based poster). The sacred space once saved solely for published works of literature is now shared with the writings of my students. While I realize that such a move was done to accommodate the reality of my students' abilities as readers, I want as well to state that this is for me an altogether admirable change. Rather than treating literature as objects of worship (I recall my Shakespeare professor bowing his head in respect at the start of our discussion of *King Lear*), such works are presented as made by men and women, whose extraordinary work is derived from the writers' often ordinary lives.

While my students' insistence that I keep things "real" has affected me dramatically, I am no less affected by but what I perceive as similar demands from colleagues. In ways subtle and not so subtle, colleagues have sent messages that reading and talking about scholarly matters smack of elitism and irrelevancy. Outside of the writing center, which has hosted various summer workshops and staff meetings on writing and thinking in the disciplines, and departmental efforts at developing learning outcomes, I have rarely witnessed campus discussions on scholarly or theoretical matters. Meetings typically are taken up with procedural or logistical affairs (whether to enroll minors in our courses or award credits to students on the basis of prior experience in a field). All such meetings are geared toward serving students and institutions efficiently and practically. Attendance at professional conferences—not a given among colleagues—is often seen as distracting faculty from the real work of teaching students. Publication, not counting toward tenure or promotion at our college, is similarly viewed as precious and not really connected to classroom instruction, even though I and others make it a point to engage in classroom research for publication. Can research and publication enhance our teaching? I believe so. Can theory inform practice and practice shape theory? Absolutely. Community college faculty need to see themselves as pedagogical researchers—needing to understand their own students more fully, apprehend the impact of their own teaching practices on student learning, and thoughtfully revise those practices in the light of such research (Tinberg, Duffy, and Mino). We have nothing to fear from intellectual inquiry and everything to gain. This study, I hope, offers a model for such inquiry: rooted in sound theory, supported by the authentic experience of students' writing.

Jean-Paul Nadeau's Narrative

Both of my parents were educators, and I was consistently encouraged to achieve excellence both in and out of school. This encouragement was explicit at times, though they also taught by example. While their official jobs weren't all that exciting, as music teachers in an elementary school and a middle school, their singing talents had led them to some acclaim. They met, in fact, in the 1960s as Fulbright scholars in Germany where they performed opera together—not the typical love story. Once they'd returned to the United States and settled in southeastern Massachusetts, they became fairly well known, having played lead roles in numerous musicals and other performances.

Attending one particular performance of one of my parents was a special experience. Sitting in the loft of Saint Mathieu's Cathedral in Fall River at midnight mass and hearing my father's bass voice boom across every surface and into every heart gave me chills. This experience and others like it kindled my own desire to affect others in a meaningful way. While I could sing, I felt (and feel) that my talents paled in comparison, and that I'd need to discover what I had to offer—how I, too, could boom. Though I spent time in various choruses and even began singing solos myself at midnight mass, I felt a sense of urgency to discover my own special talent, my calling. Many of my students, I believe, long having heard what they aren't capable of doing, are themselves on such a quest.

Other lessons emerged from hard work, in the form of manual labor at my father's right hand. Together we built sheds, erected fences, tore down and built decks, finished basements, demolished walls, tiled floors, installed pools, shingled roofs, erected three-season rooms, painted interiors, planted countless gardens, chopped down trees, shoveled, raked, hammered, cut, tightened, leveled, cemented, and sanded for more than twenty years. Long, tireless hours taught me resiliency and appreciation for downtime. My layman status taught me humility and how much I had yet to understand. My father's refusal to admit defeat taught me the value of persistence and to expect success. Goals were consistently achieved. Change was inevitable.

My secondary education, completed in 1986, emphasized the study of literature over writing, and when I was asked to write, I was required to complete a two-stage sequence. After a two-week segment of public speaking in high school, I was finally able to be myself while communicating formally. I firmly believe it was the positive experiences during that brief time that excited me about delivering a message effectively. My classmates and I had to deliver several speeches, and I put a great amount of effort into selecting a topic, message, and the means by which I'd deliver that message. I cared how my audience would respond and loved that I could immediately garner their reactions. Here I began to bloom; perhaps this is why I am so eager to share students' writing in class and to encourage verbal response.

Attending college wasn't a decision so much as the next logical step in my education: fastening the deck treads to the floor joists, so to speak. By junior year, it was clear my deck would be safer with a railing: graduate school. My parents had both been there, so not an eyebrow was raised when I steered away from employment back toward academia. This made perfect sense to my parents and me. I now, of course, understand how different this experience is from that of many of my students for whom college was costly, not only in terms of tuition and fees, but in terms of delaying (or temporarily reducing) income.

Like most of my students, I worked while attending college. While I began with a modest fifteen hour per week schedule, I had soon cobbled together a few part-time positions that equated a full-time, forty-plus hour per week work schedule. My workday as a personal trainer at a local gym began at 6:00 A.M. From there it was off to school. Classes were followed by several hours working in a video store and then four more hours as a supermarket stockperson. Such a schedule required me to use my free time wisely, though my schoolwork suffered as a result of this juggling act.

In the early 1990s, fresh out of a master's degree program in English, I considered myself lucky to be able to teach a college course—and woefully unprepared. I hadn't taken a single course to prepare for teaching at any level. After teaching part time for a couple of semesters while simultaneously enrolled in a doctoral program at the University of Rhode Island, a position opened in Bristol's Center for Developmental Education Writing Lab. I was truly fortunate to be hired in this position, where I worked as a full-time writing tutor for students in the College's Quest program for at-risk students. This work, as I will soon explain, greatly influenced the way I interact with students.

Having worked in writing centers and labs as long as I've been teaching, writing center theory grounds my pedagogy. To develop as writers, students need respectful readers of their work, readers attentive to the writing situation and the intent/goal of the author(s). My pedagogy is informed, as well, by writing center practice, specifically my own experiences as a writing center tutor. Though students, for example, often want to consider surface features of their text, time is often better spent diving deeper: into areas such as rhetorical strategies and genre-related concerns. Where to go next is a negotiation in a tutoring session and can (and should) be as well in a writing classroom or written response.

My most valuable professional development moments have involved on-campus discussions with faculty through the Center for Teaching and Learning and the Writing Center—here I gained deeper insight into students' needs, teaching possibilities, and reflective practice in general. I change assignments significantly and often, in part because I believe my response to the subject matter will affect student response. My assignments also change in an attempt to engage students with relevant and meaningful subjects and genres. I can recall the assignments that engaged me as a student—those that allowed me to attain some measure of authority despite my youth and inexperience, those where I was able to connect with readers about a subject with which I was keenly involved. New assignments allow me to look at my students' attempts at communication without comparing this class's attempts with those of past semesters.

In class, I like to spend time looking in depth at student writing in progress. Together we debate strengths and possible areas for further development. In this context, my hope is that students will learn to better anticipate how diverse readers might respond to their work. While class time helps students reflect upon their own writing processes, it is through written feedback on drafts where I feel I do most of my teaching. I consider feedback a work in progress, as I am learning to respond to a changing audience—to listen more closely and consistently—with each new semester and each new group of students. My success in this regard is gauged, in part, by students' responses to the feedback offered, particularly their responses in the form of a subsequent draft. Brian Huot, Bob Broad, and Chris Anson are among those who have helped me to understand why those who teach composition need to examine carefully the way in which they assign, read, and respond to written work—whether as individual pieces or as a collective portfolio.

Looking back, I imagine it was in the developmental writing lab where I acquired an interest in the feedback method. In the lab, I was helping students meet their professors' expectations for each assignment while I was also coming to terms with those expectations. I was able to experience, on a daily basis, the way another professor responded to student writing. As a new instructor, I found this useful, as I was eager to know whether my comments were "appropriate," whether I was focused on the most important issues in student writing, whether I was saying *enough* in response to students' written work. Was I being too demanding, or was I expecting too little from my students? Was I encouraging students to see their text as a whole, as Nancy Sommers reminds me to do, or was I creating a nonhierarchical list of errors? Was I allowing students to maintain ownership of their work? Through additional writing center experiences, both as a faculty tutor at Bristol's Writing Lab and as the associate director of Bryant's Writing Center, I gained further insight into the challenges involved in conveying expectations through assignment design and written feedback.

My teaching has also, more recently, been informed through my work at Bryant University (before I arrived at Bristol) as co-coordinator of a first-year success program, an experience that helped me better understand the challenges students face as they transition to college. What I learned from retention studies and psychological theory informed my teaching practice. One key change was that I brought challenges to the surface in and out of the classroom, letting students know that I was empathetic and eager to assist them with their development. I now, for example, suggest ways to avoid procrastination—and stress—by breaking up the work into manageable units. After teaching the first-year success course that encouraged students to employ college-level study techniques, I quickly became aware of their resistance to changing the way they studied. After all, they were in college, had used those techniques to get here, and saw college as a continuation of high school.

Because expectations and the level of challenge are higher in college, I talk with my Bristol students throughout the semester about having the humility to recognize when a method isn't working and make the necessary changes. I explain that engaging in the same activities will likely produce similar results. As we read and discuss new techniques, I ask students to give them a try and to recognize that proficiency comes with practice. By the end of the semester, most students are able to reflect upon the changes they made—including which did and didn't work—in their portfolio cover letters.

Since I first began teaching writing, I have used a shared content model to form a basis for class discussion and group brainstorming. Early on I adopted a cultural studies approach, asking students to consider the ways their identity had been constructed by various social institutions. More recently I focus on the ways in which students have been constructed as students, with some assignments that ask them to consider their attitudes and behaviors relative to education. One such assignment, for example, asks students to write a letter to next semester's incoming class to offer them academic advice. This exercise asks students to reflect upon their own successes as well as to admit having made some less than ideal choices. Another paper, this one assigned in a basic writing course, requires students to tell the story of their first day on campus.

Such assignments are, in part, an attempt to get at students' understanding of their new academic environment. Overall, students seem eager to discuss this challenging time in their lives, although many aren't used to engaging in such reflection. This study allowed me to get a much broader and deeper look into the academic experiences of community college students. After listening to them, I am encouraged to continue to respect the individuals who inhabit my rosters and to continue to adapt my instructional methods, assignments, and feedback to a changing audience.

RESEARCHING STUDENT WRITING SCIENTIFICALLY

Systematic and wide-ranging research of student writing in a school setting began in the 1960s with Albert R. Kitzhaber's report on the state of writing instruction at Dartmouth College. Kitzhaber claimed to answer some core questions. Did the students' writing in the universally required first year of composition (in Dartmouth's case, English 1 and 2, a literature-based and a theme-based course requiring research) improve when they took the courses? If so, in what way? How do we know this to be the case? What's noteworthy about Kitzhaber's study is that it regarded the close and rigorous examination of student writing (over 380,000 words of it) and teacher commentary as essential to evaluating what students learned in first-year composition.

Kitzhaber chose to focus on the written product, to which he applied formalistic categories of error, from focus and structure to punctuation and mechanics. He did not attempt to uncover the processes by which writers compose, nor did he gauge students' expectations about the work. That process- and writer-centered approach was enacted in the next decade, with publication of Janet Emig's study of twelfth-grade writers and of the Schools Council Project in the United Kingdom on the writing of eleven- through eighteen-year-olds (Britton et al.).

Emig's study aimed to produce depth rather than breadth of understanding. Her case study of Lynn, a high school student in the top 5 percent of her class, shows us a writer engaging in a range of written forms (through a series of drafts), from a profile of an intriguing person and writer's autobiography to a poem and critical analysis of Ahab in *Moby Dick*. Through interviews, logs, and composing-aloud protocol, Emig presents a thick description of Lynn's behavior as a writer. Emig documents Lynn's "profound concern for her reader" as well as Lynn's sensitivity to stylistic nuance (64, 68). Lynn is a particularly adept student, articulate and self-aware regarding her composing processes. Through examining Lynn's work and processes and those of seven other twelfth graders, Emig concluded that the schools do little to encourage what she refers to as "reflexive" writing, such as journals and diaries. Instead, too much time in school is spent on mastering "extensive" forms, such as the five-paragraph theme, that serve a purely transactional purpose and are "other-centered" (97).

While recognizing the need to treat the writing of their research cohort as significant evidence of student learning, James Britton and his colleagues placed equal emphasis on process. Following Janet Emig's study, Britton et al. aimed, like Emig, to externalize students' thinking processes as they compose: through observation, through taped "thinking aloud" sessions as children write, and through interviews of children regarding the process of writing. Despite the shared emphasis on process, the results that were reported focus on what the products or writing samples reveal: namely that writing may be usefully categorized in terms of function (expressive, transactional, and poetic) and that function exits in a reciprocal relationship with the audience (Britton 88–90, 183).

The work of Emig and Britton sends a clear message to the profession: to understand the needs of student writers, we must spend time with the writing and the writer. Both also convey the view that such research can be and ought to be conducted on a scientific basis, while at the same time grounded in specific writing situations. A tension existed from the start, therefore, between the goal of producing replicable, well-designed research studies and the goal of reproducing the specific and localized scene of writing. As composition takes a social turn in the 1980s, the latter receives considerable attention, aided by the valuable work of sociolinguists William Labov and Shirley Brice Heath, whose work, respectively, on nonstandard dialects and community-based literacies, together with the pioneering work on Black English by rhetorician Geneva Smitherman, complicates and enriches our understanding of what our students bring into the classroom.

SHAUGHNESSY, OPEN ADMISSIONS, AND DIVERSE LITERACIES

That understanding had been assisted immeasurably by the groundbreaking work of Mina Shaughnessy, whose painstaking analysis of student placement essays led so many to regard the work of teaching basic writers as a serious academic pursuit. Regardless of whether we regard Shaughnessy's analysis as too focused on "correctness" (chapter titles include "Syntax," "Spelling," and "Common Errors"), her advice that we study the "logic" of student error resonates with our study and with that of so many others. Shaughnessy offers us wise guidance when she promotes in all teachers a "readiness to look at these problems in a way that does not ignore the linguistic sophistication of the students nor yet underestimates the complexity of the task they face as they set about learning to write for college" (13). We regard these as watchwords for our current project. We also take to heart Shaughnessy's attention to underprepared writers, whose entrance during the "open admissions" experiment of the 1970s was so dramatic. As teacher/researchers working in an open admission, public, two-year college, we aspire to carry on Shaughnessy's legacy.

While composition during the 1980s turned its gaze to communities outside of the classroom—for example, nineteenth-century women's clubs in Anne Gere's work or the three Carolina towns in Shirley Brice Heath's ethnography—another group of teacher/researchers looked long and hard at the composing process and written products of undergraduate writers. Mike Rose employed a case study approach to study writer's block and Andrea Lunsford examined hundreds of student essays to ascertain stylistic features and content characteristics of basic writers, while Linda Flower and John Hayes asked student writers to narrate aloud their planning process, allowing researchers to examine the role of cognition in composing. Nancy Sommers surveyed both student writers and experienced writers to gain access to the difference in revision strategies between the two. Sommers' study ushered in a series of important studies of student writing in relation to the revision process (Beach; Flower, Hayes, et al.).

The impetus to examine student writing within naturalized settings led researchers in the 1990s to consider writers' work in response to disciplinarily specific demands. The research of Barbara Walvoord and Lucille McCarthy merit special attention in that it attempts to capture the specialized demands of particular disciplines and makes an overarching argument as to what thinking and writing are like in college. Working with "teacher-collaborators" in business, history, social science, and biology, Walvoord and McCarthy account for both the differences and similarities in faculty expectations among these four disciplines. A careful examination of writing tasks and students' written products yields the observation that student writers are more likely to behave as "text processors" (summarizing or recapitulating reading or lectures) rather than defining a stance of their own; moreover, they might write without concern for an audience rather than shape their writing to an audience of peers as "practitioners in training" might--learning what it means, for example, to do the work of a biologist or historian (102, 153). Engaging undergraduates and faculty in a conversation about what it takes to think and write in the disciplines can only enhance understanding of teaching and learning, although disciplinary conventions are hardly static. In fact, as a recent empirical study has shown, such conventions are likely to be moving targets. Chris Thais and Terry Myers Zawacki report a "degree of contentiousness" in some disciplines regarding the use of alternative genres, for example (42).

The current study, while indebted to previous research on students' struggle to find their disciplinary footing, focuses on the writing of first-semester community college students who, while having declared only a broad field of concentration (such as "business" or "communications"), are really at the very earliest stages of adapting to college writing demands and thus are likely not to have been exposed to highly specialized genres and audiences. It is also worthwhile to note that, given our short time frame of one semester, any claims of development need to be tempered. As Richard Haswell suggests in his study of placement essays of first-year composition students and advanced composition students, such claims need to be carefully thought through (*Gaining*). In fact, Haswell argues, we too often misinterpret the writing of experienced writers by applying standards applicable to novices only. While we attempt to chart the changes that students make over several drafts, our purpose here is primarily descriptive: we intend to account for the nature of students' writing tasks at college—and the degree of success achieved in meeting the writing challenge.

THE FIRST YEAR OF COLLEGE:
THE VIEW FROM HARVARD

The first semester of college, which is the focus of this study, is that crucial period of time in which, as Nancy Sommers and Laura Saltz observe, students experience the "paradox of . . . writing simultaneously as a novice and an expert" (132). Students are often asked to engage in the conventions of academic disciplines without a clear road map, or as one Harvard student tells Sommers and Saltz, "She was being asked 'to build a house without any tools'" (131). The challenges are enormous: "Students are pushed to practice the new conventions of college writing: to consider questions for which they don't have answers, or to write for readers who aren't already converted to their way of thinking, and to accept their own minds as capable of synthesizing and making judgments about dense ideas" (133).

Prior writing experiences in a first-year composition class, as Lee Ann Carroll's study of undergraduate writing at Pepperdine has shown, "do not directly transfer to students' work in their major areas of study" (9). Yet it's the very pressure of being a novice that leads so many students to achieve expertise and to see a "greater purpose in writing than completing an assignment" (Sommers and Saltz 139). Such progress stands a better chance of being realized when "faculty treat freshmen as apprentice scholars" and relieve "students of the responsibility of inventing the field for themselves" (140, 138). These conclusions are among many significant findings in the Harvard Study of Undergraduate Writing led by Sommers and Saltz. Having followed more than 400 students in the Harvard class of 2001 through to graduation, Sommers and her research team sifted through considerable survey data, 520 hours of interviews, and over 600 pounds of student writing. The Harvard study, while committed to understanding what undergraduate writing says about student learning, is equally committed to telling students' stories and allowing students' own accounts of their journey from novice to experienced writer.

CONSTRUCTING THE WRITER

Our analysis, beyond being descriptive of the writing, will also attempt to construct the figure of the writer herself. We recognize, as do researchers such as Marilyn Sternglass and Anne Herrington and Marcia Curtis, that a systematic study of undergraduate writing must take into account not only the writing practices of students but also a consideration of the life-world challenges that each writer faces. This is especially so with community college students, for whom the paths to success are so often blocked by formidable barriers. Many of the students whom we get to know in this study face the same daunting challenges as Marcia Curtis's basic writing students: "In the essays of basic writers . . . , I often saw expressed—either implicitly through form or explicitly through content—much of the same fragmentation, isolation, alienation, helplessness, and anger that therapists reported their clients were bringing with them to their sessions" (Herrington and Curtis 25). But we do them an injustice if we construct these writers through deficit models only because these students' stories often reveal considerable resilience and a determination to succeed.

Our study intends to give voice to students who have yet to be heard: community college writers. While article-length analyses of community college student writers have been published, most notably in the national journal *Teaching English in the Two-Year College*, not one full-length study of undergraduate writing that we know of has included either the available scholarship on the subject or new work on these students. Kitzhaber is to be excused when in 1963 he gathered composition syllabi from ninety-five colleges and universities but noted the "absence of junior colleges" to his otherwise "fairly representative cross section of American institutions of higher education" (9). After all, the boom in community and junior colleges had not quite yet happened (although junior colleges had been in existence for over half a century). The greater shame is that today, with a near majority of undergraduates currently enrolled in community colleges, large-scale research focusing on student writers continues to neglect this significant population.

We hope to begin to fill that gap. We will do so, to a great degree, by letting these students speak for themselves. In so doing, we seek to avoid what Kurt Spellmeyer has called "profoundly dishonest— constructions of the student and the student's language" (quoted in Herrington and Curtis 43). Our students have stories to tell and we intend to let them tell those stories. Too often community colleges and the students who attend them are mischaracterized and reduced to simplistic stereotypes (students who cared little about high school and care even less about college or those who opt for community college because it poses few challenges). This is their time to set the record straight.

2

Design and Method

IN THE SPRING SEMESTER OF 2007, we administered a survey of our college faculty—in both online and hard copy versions—to determine faculty expectations regarding student writing and preferred modes of response to student work. This was the first survey we were to administer as part of the study, so we wanted to do so in a way that allowed for respondents to complete the form easily and conveniently while also easing the data input process. We knew the number of faculty surveys would be significantly fewer in number than the student surveys we'd soon be administering, so we intended to streamline the surveying process using our experiences from this smaller set of data.

The initial plan was to go with an online survey only. We met with a member of the College's information technology department for his expert assistance in putting the survey online and helping us reach our target population. To accomplish the latter, we decided to use the college's web portal, AccessBCC, to which each faculty member, and student for that matter, has username and password access. Putting the survey onto AccessBCC was the first step, but we needed to ask faculty to complete the survey and to make sure they had easy access. We communicated this request via a campus e-mail to the full- and part-time faculty listservs.

Once the online survey was live and the request sent, we waited two weeks for faculty to respond. At about the time of our survey, the campus library was administering its own comprehensive online survey, and were dangling a carrot: completing a survey meant entering a drawing to win an Apple iPod. Would we be able to compete for the limited time faculty had available? The completed surveys trickled in a handful every few days as we eagerly and anxiously logged in to check the numbers. After two weeks, the grand total was twenty-five completed surveys, not enough to make any generalizations. It seemed that demands upon faculty were working against us.

We switched to "plan B." Each division of the college meets monthly, and we decided to take advantage of the next such meeting to gather the data we needed. Since these meetings took place in meeting rooms and large classrooms with a single computer only, we created hard copy versions of the faculty survey (appendix C) and asked the deans of each division if they would assist us by administering the surveys during the meeting. This method was more successful, likely because faculty had time to complete the survey. There may also have been some faculty who couldn't access or were resistant to using the online version.

Seventy faculty members responded in total, twenty-five through the online form and forty-five via hard copy. Of the forty-five who filled out the hard copy, forty identified themselves as full time; unfortunately, no such opportunity to identify themselves was given on the online version. The preponderance of full-time faculty was no doubt a reflection of the makeup of division meetings, which typically have few part-time faculty in attendance. The following departments were represented: accounting, biology, computer information, criminal justice, culinary arts, engineering, English, history, management, office science, math, nursing, psychology, and sociology. A self-study report conducted in 2004 reveals that there were 98 full-time and 250 part-time faculty in the fall of 2002 ("NEASC" 43). These numbers provided a fair estimate of the current size of the faculty, meaning approximately 20 percent of the full-time faculty responded to our survey.

Faculty were asked to respond to thirty-one statements, using a five-point scale ranging from strongly disagree to strongly agree. Several statements focused on faculty perceptions of the role of writing for students, how students perceive themselves as writers, the potential for writing skill development on the part of students, and students' motivation toward developing as writers. Related statements questioned whether writing is discussed during class meeting time.

A significant number of statements in the survey focused on faculty perceptions of their students' writing habits. Some statements were included to indicate whether there were some writing practices faculty thought were important for students, such as brainstorming, seeking feedback, and rereading the paper. Other statements revealed the opposite: those practices of students that faculty thought were not helpful, such as focusing too much on grammatical issues during the revision process.

Another set of statements required respondents to reflect upon their response practice. We wanted to know whether faculty thought the process led to stronger writing—whether the precious time invested was productive and educational—and whether faculty offered feedback on drafts in progress. Several statements focused on the form such responses take. Here we hoped to gain some insight into the rationale behind response methods, an understanding we could deepen with upcoming faculty interviews and the feedback we'd be able to review on the papers written by our student cohort.

Finally, we asked faculty to consider their expectations for student writing. Among the statements in this vein were several that asked about the level of challenge. One statement asked whether students were well prepared for challenging writing assignments at the start of the course, and one asked whether students were well prepared at the end of the course. Here we hoped to understand if faculty thought they were helping students develop their writing skills.

SELECTING A FACULTY COHORT

In contrast with other longitudinal studies of student writers such as that of Herrington and Curtis that interviewed a faculty of cohort participants, we chose to interview a representative sampling of Bristol's faculty. Faculty were selected from across the college's six divisions, and each is represented: Humanities and Education; Behavioral and Social Sciences; Business and Information Management; Health Sciences; Mathematics, Science, Engineering; and the Center for Developmental Education. The eleven individuals interviewed included eight full-time and three part-time faculty. Four were male and seven female. We talked with individuals from numerous programs: human services, English, English as a second language, graphic design, occupational therapy, history, nursing, accounting, economics, communications, and developmental math. Instead of randomly selecting faculty, we selected those we knew were assigning writing in their courses, knowledge gleaned from our affiliation with the campus writing lab. Our reasoning was that if we were to better understand the types and amounts of writing assigned, we should focus on those faculty who currently assign and respond to writing in their courses.

FACULTY INTERVIEWS

To deepen our understanding of the survey findings, one-on-one interviews, lasting an average of forty-five minutes, were conducted with each of the members of the faculty cohort during the spring 2007 semester. Interview questions were standardized (appendix D), although interviews weren't conducted in a rigid manner, allowing for discussions that resulted, on occasion, in questions being addressed out of order.

Some questions focused on the values that individual faculty members attached to good student writing, values that at times were generalized, at times specific to particular disciplines and programs. Other questions asked faculty to reflect upon their students' attitudes about writing. Faculty also described the particulars of various writing assignments they used in their courses as well as the rationale behind, and consequences of, their methods of responding to students' written work.

THE STUDENT FOCUS GROUP

Next, we began the process of obtaining feedback from students themselves. While drafting the student survey and initial interview questions, we thought it important to involve students in the process to make sure we were asking the right questions in terms of past experience and expectations. During the spring 2007 semester, with the assistance of a full-time member of the English department, we met students in a single section of College Writing, our college's required writing course. The fifty-minute discussion was videotaped and subsequently transcribed. Students' responses were carefully considered, and questions were added or modified accordingly.

One recurring theme during the focus group was students' disdain for writing "formulas" that they had had to follow in high school, including the "five by five" method. We decided to add a question to the initial interview that asked students whether they were surprised by anything they were learning through their college writing instruction. With this question, we hoped to discover whether such formulas had a limited shelf life or were encouraged by college faculty. Of course, it would help to uncover other incongruities as well; one thing our focus group helped us to understand was that students were hoping college would offer an experience fundamentally different from that of high school.

THE STUDENT SURVEY

In the fall of 2007, we administered a hard-copy survey to first-time students at four two-year colleges. While our focus is on the local population at Bristol, we sought to contextualize our findings and draw some generalizations. We wondered whether Bristol students responded in a manner consistent with other two-year college students throughout the nation. First-semester students were surveyed at the three other institutions, Santa Barbara City College in California, Illinois Central College in Peoria, Illinois, and Whatcom Community College in Bellingham, Washington.

At Bristol, 337 first-time students completed the survey, a sample size representing one-third of the 1,031 first-time students attending the college that semester. Faculty who were teaching courses traditionally populated by first-semester students assisted us by administering the survey. The instrument consisted of twenty-seven statements to be responded to via a Likert scale ranging from strongly disagree to strongly agree, indicating the extent to which respondents believed each statement to be true.

The survey (appendix B) aimed to get at a range of student perceptions but emphasized three in particular: students' attitudes about

NORTHEAST WISCONSIN TECHNICAL COLLEGE
LEARNING RESOURCE CENTER
MARINETTE, WI 54143

writing, perceptions of their own writing processes, and experiences in high school relative to writing instruction.

A good number of those statements were designed to gauge students' expectations about writing instruction as they began their college careers, in particular those attitudes that would likely influence their ability to develop writing skills in college courses. "I am a strong writer" and "I can develop my writing skills" are statements that should help us understand whether students are open to others' suggestions regarding drafts or whether they express more of an external locus of control and feel that their writing skills are as strong as others say.

Still another set of statements asked respondents to reflect upon past writing processes and instructional techniques, some getting at familiarity and others at efficacy. Statements like "I produce more than one draft before submitting a paper to my teacher" and "I show my writing to someone before handing it to a teacher," for example, were intended to gather insight about whether students would have experience with drafting, whether that process involved surface editing or soliciting feedback from others and adjusting support accordingly.

Another set of statements required students to reflect upon their high school experiences. It seemed logical that recent instructional approaches to writing would influence students' attitudes toward approaches used in college. Here we asked students to gauge agreement with statements like "In my high school writing courses, I had to revise my work using classmates' feedback on drafts" and "In my high school writing courses, I commented on other students' papers" to understand whether our students were familiar with peer review. One of the more important statements included students' assessment of their previous high school writing instruction: "My high school writing instruction prepared me to write papers in college." Perhaps an equally important statement was included in response to a too common refrain of students: that they haven't had experience writing research papers. Students were asked to agree or disagree that: "In high school I wrote papers using research." While there were other areas to explore, we thought it best to be realistic in terms of survey length. We were looking for completed surveys from a statistically significant number of students.

SELECTING A STUDENT COHORT

In the next phase, we probed deeper to study individual student writers at our institution over an extended period, that important first semester. To do so, we needed to select a group of students and contact them about participation before they arrived on campus. This was tricky, as we needed to select randomly a representative group from a necessarily incomplete list of fall 2007 BCC students, as students are allowed to enroll in courses several days into the official start of the semester.

To acquire the random list needed, we met with the vice president of institutional research, who, over several meetings, was able to help us determine which variables to use when sorting student records. We could then use the college's Banner Information System to randomly select students meeting our criteria.

We had to define what we meant by "new first-semester BCC student." Would we include only students enrolled in a program? Would transfer students be allowed to be part of the group? Did we want only students with zero college credits? If so, what would we do about students who had taken noncredit courses? We eventually decided to exclude students who had transferred to BCC having taken college classes elsewhere, as we believed these students' understanding of college writing would have been influenced by their prior college experiences. Students with zero credits earned and a GPA of zero would be included on the list. We wanted a range of student programs, including students in nondegree programs, as well. In brief, we wanted to focus on students for whom BCC would be the first college experience.

The vice president of institutional research produced a list of forty-five student names. Because this group was random, we reasoned that there would be a representative breakdown in terms of gender, full/part-time status, English language learners, program of study, and developmental needs. We optimistically anticipated working with two-thirds of this group, or approximately thirty students, at the start and, through inevitable attrition, eventually about twenty students. We needed to contact these forty-five students to inform them about the study and ask for their participation.

CONSTRUCTING THE STUDENT COHORT

Each of the students was sent a letter inviting them to a two-hour orientation meeting and lunch before the start of classes. The letter outlined the benefits of participation as well as what we would be asking from participants. We promised lunch as an added incentive as well as a gift gas card to ameliorate rising gas prices as an obstacle to attendance. Students were asked to let us know whether they'd be attending; only ten did so.

The orientation meeting was conducted before the start of classes and before the college's official student orientation. We hoped that this time slot would find students more flexible, perhaps while they were on campus to buy books, pay bills, and conduct other last-minute errands. At the orientation, we planned to describe the project and what we'd be asking of participants, offer students the opportunity to sign the project consent form, have attendees complete the student survey, and explain the writing collection process. We wanted to share our excitement about the project and help students understand the significance of their participation, enhancing the learning of the student writers to follow. We were eager to meet with and hear from them, to help them navigate their first days of college. To our disappointment, only six students attended the meeting.

We needed a larger sample to study. With the start of the semester looming and our project timeline in danger, we decided to enlist participants in several ways. If our goal was to finish the study with twenty or so students, we'd need to do more recruiting. First, we wanted to follow up with students who received our original letter to determine if they were interested in being part of the study despite not having attended the orientation. Our initial step would be to call and e-mail the thirty-nine nonattendees to request that they schedule individual informational meetings, at which time we'd also have them complete the required paperwork: (1) reviewing, discussing, and signing a consent form for the study, (2) completing a student survey, and (3) supplying accurate contact information. Through this method we were able to add a handful of students to the cohort, bringing the total to ten. We were into double digits and making progress, but we were still only halfway to our goal.

Once we'd made this effort to engage the initial group of forty-five, we asked for a second list of possible participants from the vice president of institutional research. With approximately twice the number of potential participants, we thought we'd be able to achieve our target cohort size. We received the second list less than a week after making our request; because of this, we could ensure that these students would still be new to the college experience. A letter of invitation was sent and e-mailed to these eighty-five students.

In the interim, student orientation took place, and we saw this as an opportunity to solicit additional participants. On this day, one of us approached students on campus, explaining the study and asking whether they'd like to be involved. If so, their contact information was recorded, and these fifteen students received phone calls and e-mails in the next few days, asking them to stop in for a brief orientation. Multiple attempts were made to contact students. In total, with the students who were approached at orientation, the the second list of eighty-five, and our original group of ten, twenty students eventually met with us for an orientation. Four didn't persist beyond that point.

The end result of our recruitment efforts was a diverse cohort consisting of sixteen students (appendix A, with one student having dropped out). Two of the sixteen were male. Four were returning students. Five of the students categorized themselves as ethnic minorities, one as a noncitizen. Six were part-time students during the fall semester, and eight took at least one developmental course during that time. Three students had at least one dependent other than their spouse living at home. Three were taking courses exclusively at one of Bristol's satellite campuses, and three others were taking courses only in the evening.

After looking closely at this group that was gathered through weeks of phone calls and e-mails, we became aware of a complication. Despite our efforts to include only zero credit, zero GPA students in the study, several students fell through the cracks of our spreadsheet. Three had taken a single course at BCC during the summer 2007 semester, and another student had taken a course some time ago at another community college. Because of the difficulty involved with solidifying and retaining a cohort, we decided to resolve this issue by adjusting questions for these individuals as opposed to rejecting valuable participants. For the students who took summer courses, we asked them to reflect back upon their mindset before the courses; for the student who had studied at another institution, her experience was so limited and distant that, of her own admission, it didn't significantly affect her perception of college writing.

Yet another complication was that three of the students in the cohort were enrolled in courses being taught by one of the researchers that fall. Again, we decided to allow the students to participate in the study, and to analyze each others' students' writing, interview, and survey data to avoid the potential for bias. Our connection with these individuals, we hoped, would help retain them in the study, a primary concern.

INITIAL INTERVIEW

Depending on student preference and availability, the initial interview was scheduled at, or conducted toward the end of, the orientation session. Each interview was scheduled for a half hour. The interviews were digitally recorded and transcribed.

As part of the interview (appendix E), each student was asked to describe his or her writing ability and to discuss the amount and types of writing done in high school. We asked students to explain what makes for an effective paper and how they go about working toward that goal. Along those lines, one question was devoted exclusively to students' experiences writing research papers. We also asked students to recall the most useful feedback they'd received on a paper from a teacher. In addition to reflecting upon past practices, we asked students how much and what kinds of writing they expected to do as a college student.

In retrospect, the interviews were fairly brief, and we hypothesize that this was the case for several reasons. Students' schedules placed severe limitations on interview time—many squeezed in their interviews between classes, before leaving school for work, or upon arriving for night classes after a full day of work. Particularly during this first interview, students weren't familiar with us, and, combined with our attempt to avoid offering our own thoughts about writing and challenges ahead, may have been reticent to fully engage our questions. There were other reasons students may have been unable to discuss their writing practices and experiences with us, including a limited vocabulary regarding the subject.

Other students were concise for more practical reasons. One interview, for example, was with Anne Marie. She arrived at her orientation meeting with her one-year-old son in a stroller. Since she was taking classes online and was rarely on campus, she wanted to know if we could conduct the initial interview immediately after the orientation. We complied, with underwhelming results.

The interview lasted only ten minutes or so. Her son had lost his patience by that point, and who would blame him? Anne Marie was forced to hold him, pace, and dodge an occasional blow to her head while being bombarded by difficult questions. Her responses were relatively abrupt, in comparison to those of other respondents, and it seemed the situation had limited her ability to engage in the careful reflection the questions required. We were asking her, after all, to reflect back on high school and predict the future, neither easy tasks even without such a distraction.

Indeed, these questions were challenging for all cohort participants in that they required the use of powers of recall and prediction in regards to a subject they may not have given much thought. Students may have been intimidated by this demanding task, perhaps perceiving it as a test given by a relatively unknown authority figure.

SECOND STUDENT INTERVIEW

Toward the end of the semester, we conducted a second interview with cohort participants to see whether their expectations for the first semester meshed with their actual experience. Having had nine or ten weeks of college student experience, they were now in a position to do so. While the initial interviews had focused on experiences in high school, now we were able to get more specific about experiences with college-level writing. Here we were interested in whether there had been any change in students' attitudes and behaviors related to writing as well as what may have prompted such change, including instructor feedback.

Students were asked a series of eight questions (appendix F) that attempted to explore how writing was used in the courses students were enrolled in as well as how they responded to the writing. Having previously asked about students' writing processes, we were curious as to whether there had been any changes. Had their first semester of college writing instruction encouraged them to write differently? Had they developed their vocabulary to be able to talk more specifically about the way they write? If they had made changes to their writing processes, were these changes at least in part the result of being asked to write in new genres? Or, perhaps, were these changes a result of demands to be more analytical? We were also interested in whether students thought their writing skills had improved. Here we were asking them to evaluate the writing instruction they'd received as well as their own response—in terms of motivation, risk taking, and other factors—to that instruction. These questions asked students to rely on their metacognitive ability, a skill that some students had developed more than others. Finally, several questions focused on faculty response. We wanted to know whether students had seen any trends in the feedback they'd received, whether there had been any pleasant or unpleasant surprises, and whether they'd noticed a difference in the way their high school teachers and college professors responded to their writing.

COLLECTION OF STUDENT WRITING

In addition to being interviewed, cohort participants were asked to submit copies of all of the writing they produced during the semester for review, a process explained during the orientation and detailed in a one-page handout. We asked students to drop off everything that would be considered writing, from class notes to lab reports to expository essays. The writing was to be dropped off at one of the researcher's offices, and a schedule of our availability, expanded for this purpose, was attached to the aforementioned handout. A copier was purchased so that students could have their writing returned promptly and with reasonable convenience. We explained that we hoped to determine whether student and professor expectations were in sync by reviewing student responses to assignments, the assignments themselves, and the comments faculty added to the writing submitted.

A substantial amount of writing was collected, though the amount varied from student to student. Some students were more consistent about dropping off their written work; others submitted only a few pieces of writing. Some students shared copies of their class notes while others did not. While we requested all writing, we suspect that, despite our repeated attempts to clarify, students submitted what *they* considered to be writing, and may have avoided submitting work they didn't want others to see. The amount of writing collected did not impact students' continued participation in the project.

A THIRD (INFORMAL) INTERVIEW: OVER LUNCH

Because of the abbreviated nature and limited scope of our inter-actions with the cohort over the course of the semester, we felt it important to contact them further—in part to get to know them and partly to allow them to discuss their first semester experience after having had more time to process. While this was one of the goals of the second interview, its timing meant that students were in the throes of projects, papers, and their first set of final exams. As classes were getting underway in the spring 2008 semester, we contacted students in the cohort to invite them to lunch and an informal postmortem, so to speak.

We had lunch with four students to help us fill in some of the gaps in terms of their first semester experiences. Our relaxed, roughly hour-long chats revolved around what brought the students to Bristol Community College, what challenges they faced while here, and what they felt enabled them to persist to this point. The students seemed more comfortable in this forum, perhaps because the focus wasn't solely on their writing attitudes and practices.

RETAINING STUDENTS IN THE COHORT

As we expected, students persisted in the study to varying degrees. Sixteen completed the student survey and consent form. Fifteen sat for the initial interview, and eleven met with one of the researchers for a second interview. Four met with us during the spring 2008 semester to discuss their college experiences and background as students.

Efforts to retain cohort participants were multifaceted. Starting with the invitation letters and orientation meetings, we stressed the benefits of participating. We considered ways to meet students' needs. The most basic needs were addressed with incentives such as a free lunch and gift gas cards. The need for safety was addressed in our providing guidance and mentoring to students as they interacted with their new environment. Realizing that students would need to feel direct benefits to remain part of the study, we arranged to have five office hours between us when we'd meet with cohort participants only. We explained that students could get feedback, as they might at the campus Writing Lab, on writing in process. They could also use these hours to check in regularly about their progress and get their questions answered as new college students.

Other students would need to feel a sense of belonging, and we hoped that participation in such a closely knit group with a common goal would provide this. Indications after our initial orientation were that this would be the case, as one student was helping an anxious peer prepare for the demands of college over lunch. Participation in the study could help other students meet their need for esteem, as they would feel part of a select group receiving sustained attention from serious researchers. Finally, those students who self-actualized would be drawn to the study by the promise of helping others enjoy a more seamless learning process.

During the fifteen-week semester, several students stayed in contact with us through the office hours we'd established, though others elected to communicate with us via e-mail only. We used e-mail to contact the group with announcements and requests periodically, in part to remind them about the study and our willingness to assist them. For students taking courses exclusively at satellite campuses, we offered to arrange for regular meeting times at the satellite location to spare them the twenty- to fifty-minute trip to the main campus. Two of these students did meet with us in this manner.

We are pleased with the outcome of our efforts. But, clearly, those efforts remind us all, if we needed such a reminder, that our students are under enormous stress as they juggle numerous responsibilities of family, work, and school—a fact that goes a long way toward explaining why this population has evaded the kind of systematic study that we advocate here. The challenges that these students face on a daily basis is very much part of the story here. At no time did we forget the struggle that so many community college students endured to get to the college. At no time did we forget the struggle that so many endure to persist.

3

What Community College Faculty Expect

WHO ARE COMMUNITY COLLEGE FACULTY?

SINCE THEIR EXPANSION IN THE 1960s, community colleges have struggled to be all things to all people—teaching students who are not prepared to do college-level work even as they provide convenient and affordable access to higher education for those who have the appropriate skills but who, because of economic necessity, have not taken or cannot take the traditional path through college.

The faculty who teach this complex cadre of students take on the rich complexity of their charge. Rather than rely, however, on reductive characterizations of community faculty, we intend to explore deeply the nature of faculty work and expectations. While our project remains firmly centered on the learning experiences of first-semester community college students, we feel that their story in this momentous first semester cannot be fully told without attending to the stories of the faculty who instruct them. In the process, we hope to paint a more accurate portrait of community college faculty than has been attempted to this point.

Nationally, who are the faculty who teach at community colleges? As of 2004, 66 percent of the faculty at public two-year colleges were part time, as compared to 36 percent at four-year colleges (public and private) and 29 percent at master's and doctorate granting institutions (TYCA, "Two-Year College Faculty Profile"). We know that among all faculty and instructional staff about 48 percent are tenured and 15 percent are on a tenure track (TYCA, "Two-Year/Four-Year Full-Time/Part-Time Tenure Status").

In terms of degree attainment, 71 percent of full-time public two-year college faculty have a master's degree while 13 percent have a doctorate ("Faculty Degree Attainment"). Among part-time faculty, 46 percent have a master's, 33 percent have a bachelor's degree, and 5 percent have doctorates ("Faculty Degree Attainment").

Pedagogical approaches among community college faculty vary considerably, as Grubb and his associates have attested. The most common, according to Grubb, remains the didactic, teacher-centered approach, in which the lecture is prominent (28). Students under this regime are often given knowledge in small bits and assessment routinely takes the form of "skill and drill" exercises. But it is possible as well to observe faculty employing a "meaning-making" or constructivist mode of teaching (31). Under this model, faculty rely on a student-centered mode, one that promotes interpretive abilities on the part of the student through considerable in-class discussion and reflective writing. Here students are offered the chance to grasp a subject in its complexity from the outset. The report on the findings of the Community College Survey of Student Engagement (CCSSE), even as it strongly recommends the use of class discussion and active learning to promote student persistence and achievement, indicates that that there is much work to be done to bring faculty aboard: "Almost a third of faculty respondents (31%) report that they spend more than half of their class time lecturing. More than one-fifth of respondents (21%) spend zero hours on small group activities . . . more than half of respondents (52%) spend less than 20% of class time on teacher-led discussion" (CCSSE). Faculty practices, however, differ radically from institution to institution, as the CCSSE reports (with some campuses making thoughtful use of supplemental instruction or web-based tools to engage students as active learners).

By focusing our research on a particular institution, Bristol Community College, and through surveys, interviews, and writing assignments of faculty who teach at the college, we hope to get beyond the numbers, to get to know community college faculty motivations and attitudes in ways that a purely statistical analysis cannot do.

INSTITUTIONAL SNAPSHOT
One of fifteen public community colleges in Massachusetts, Bristol, located in the southeastern Massachusetts town of Fall River, was

founded in December 1965, graduating its first class in June 1968 ("History of BCC"). The college, according to its Web site, offers more than ninety programs of study, offering associates degrees and certificates of achievement ("About"). Enrollment of day and evening students in credit-bearing courses falls just under 7,000 students ("About"). Tuition amounts to $123 per credit, a figure that places Bristol above the national average (TYCA, "Tuition"). According to the most recent figures published by the college, roughly 40 percent of its students receive some kind of financial aid ("About").

The college's most recent self-study report (2004) notes that "in fall 2002, more than 40% of incoming students failed the writing sample assessment . . . and more than 20% fell below the state-mandated cut off for reading" ("NEASC" 9). That same document reports that "45% failed the basic arithmetic test, and 90% did not pass the state-mandated algebra score required for placement into college-level math courses" ("NEASC" 9). Bristol is not alone in the demand for developmental instruction, however: the "remediation crisis" affects community colleges nationally, with one longitudinal study reporting that "more than 60% of first-time community college students . . . took at least one remedial course, compared to 29% of first-time students in public 4-year institutions" (Levin and Calcagno).

Regarding faculty, the same self-study report notes that in fall 2002, the college employed 98 full-time and 250 adjunct faculty. More recently, as reported by the Massachusetts Community College Council (MCCC), Bristol is reported to have 96 full-time and 381 adjunct faculty. Approximately, then, 80 percent of all faculty at the college are part time, a figure considerably higher than the 69 percent at community colleges statewide (MCCC). Full-time instructors, at Bristol and statewide, currently carry a five-course teaching load.

WHAT THE FACULTY TOLD US

Faculty Surveys

Before speaking with individual faculty about their teaching, we cast a wider net in the form of a brief survey of full- and part-time

Bristol faculty, as noted in chapter 2. Our hope was to be able to identify relationships among the statements made during one-on-one interviews and the responses of the larger group via the survey.

A review of the survey results indicated a number of areas where faculty seemed to be in agreement. For one, 80 percent thought that effective writing skills are important for student success in college and the workplace, but nearly the same number, 78 percent, thought that students didn't consider themselves to be strong writers. An even greater number, 89 percent, felt that students weren't ready to handle challenging writing assignments. These responses suggest that faculty feel there is work to be done in helping students develop their writing skills—and, perhaps, their level of confidence as writers. In fact, 90 percent affirmed students' capability of acquiring these skills. There is the suggestion here that faculty feel obligated and/or able to help promote students' success as writers. When asked, however, whether students were sufficiently prepared at the end of the course to succeed with challenging writing assignments, only 31 percent of faculty thought so. Such findings indicate that there is a need for faculty to revisit and, possibly, reconsider the way they are approaching writing instruction in their courses.

The survey inquired about such approaches, in terms of how much writing was assigned as well as how students were to proceed with writing assignments. Another important set of questions asked faculty to consider their methods of responding to student writing and their reasons for doing so. Surveys began to paint a picture, one that would be fleshed out by the interviews.

Not surprisingly, faculty who ask students to write in their courses do so in a variety of ways. Forty-three percent prefer essay exams to objective exams. Sixty-nine percent require writing that draws upon research; such writing would likely be done by students outside of the classroom. The majority, 74 percent, reported that they attempted to help students with these assignments by discussing one or more elements of the writing process with students individually or as a class.

Other responses led us to conclude that faculty ask students to do multiple assignments and/or drafts of individual assignments, as 81 percent reported that the feedback offered was helpful to students. Such a conclusion was likely drawn from perceived progress from one draft to another or from a student's response from one assignment to another. Other data supports this logic: 85 percent reported seeing improvements in student writing as a result of faculty feedback. Also interesting to note here is that 19 percent didn't see their feedback as helpful to students, and 15 percent failed to see improvement in student writing.

Approximately two-thirds of respondents reported that they offered feedback on student writing before assigning a grade. When asked about the form such feedback took, 43 percent reported offering one-on-one conferencing with students, and 53 percent reported responding to student writing electronically. Of those who offer feedback, 97 percent identify errors in grammar, diction, and mechanics.

Though a significant number of faculty require students to produce multiple drafts of their work, only 13 percent believe students are accustomed to doing so. When asked whether they expect students to produce multiple drafts, only 40 percent had this expectation. Though this seems to contradict earlier data, namely the 66 percent that reported offering feedback on student writing before assigning a grade, this response might get at something interesting. Perhaps faculty are suggesting that, despite requiring drafts, they don't expect all students to follow through—or perhaps the "drafts" wouldn't, in the professor's mind, be significantly different.

Faculty Interviews

As noted earlier, we interviewed eleven faculty. Seven came to their full-time position after having spent some time as adjunct faculty at the college. At least five of the faculty arrived at the college from the workplace: one as a graphic designer, another as an occupational therapist, a third had owned his own business, another had worked as an accountant, and another a public relations/communications director. One taught in the public schools. And one faculty arrived directly from graduate school.

All assigned considerable writing in their courses, from brief in-class responses to extended out-of-class research assignments.

Assigned genres included interviews with workplace professionals, nursing care plans and clinical self-evaluations, analyses of business operations, an ethnography of an organization's communication structure, film reviews, critiques of scholarly articles, imaginative dialogues, agency field reports, and rhetorical analyses of written argumentation. Faculty, especially those who teach in the career and technical fields, stress the importance of writing in the profession, making a strong case to their students that writing matters "out there." Consider what a human services faculty member tells his students about the impact of writing on clients and their families:

> A person might be going to a judge for some type of custody hearing, and they would very often ask the social worker . . . for a kind of evaluation. What's your opinion? Should this person be allowed to keep the kids, and if so, should it go to this parent or that parent . . . ? Or, even just something like documenting the fact that the parent that's in potential trouble has gone through the required, in some cases, parent training or anger management or whatever the heck they have to go through, the equivalent of traffic school or something like that. . . . Has the person been cooperative, attentive? Have they come to all the classes and stuff? And sometimes you just have to document stuff like that.

A faculty member in occupational therapy makes the same claim for writing in her field:

> We have such a need for clear written and oral communication skills because, for instance, if one of these students is teaching a family member about how to care for someone, they need to be able to write out very clear instructions, an information sheet. They need to give presentations. Say they work in a long-term care facility and they're teaching the nurses' aides how to [assist] somebody, which could actually really hurt someone if it isn't done correctly. They're going to be called upon to gather all of the nurses' aides on all of the shifts and to teach them, in like five or ten minutes, how to do that and

why it's important. And they also need to persuade them that they really do want to go along with doing this as part of the health care routine. And they need to leave clear instructions for everyone.

For at least one faculty, however, the reason to write well goes beyond being ready for the exigencies of the workplace. A developmental math instructor, whose assignment asks students to reflect on how they learn (what he calls the "information processing model"), views writing as an opportunity, he says, to "break down that barrier of, of looking at disciplines being separate, that you only would use English in English, you'd only use math and . . . engineering, certain applications." Writing takes on the function of explaining to students why math is as challenging as it is when compared to a subject that relies on an altogether different mode of comprehension. The faculty member poses a question and a possible answer: "Why [does] somebody like history[?] Because it tells a story." He goes on: "There's a narrative there for them, and . . . they can remember narratives for various reasons." On the other hand, he notes, "When you read a math book and they give you a generalized concept and then they start giving you specific examples, they told you something that you're really not going to understand until you . . . see the concrete examples there. See how the generalized concept comes from those [examples]."

Given the disparate motives for assigning writing and the diverse range of written genres offered to students, we thought it important to inquire of faculty as to what exactly they expect students to demonstrate in their written work. What rubrics did they employ? And to what extent were they explicit regarding their expectations for student achievement and success? Not surprisingly, given the survey results, most faculty interviewed rated a concern for technical correctness as important, if for no other reason than that it becomes difficult to access a paper's content. Here's how an accounting professor put it: "To me [faulty grammar and mechanics] make it hard for me to read. I just want something quick and legible, and brief enough to give me what I want, but if, if I don't see the punctuation, I get lost in it, and I have to keep rereading and now I have to decipher where their sentence begins and ends, so it takes a lot of time. I find that a lot with our students." Some faculty will engage themselves directly with students on such matters; others will do so to a certain extent but will in addition rely on what a human service faculty member refers to as "outsourcing" to the professional: that is, a writing center tutor to assist with grammar and mechanics.

But, to a person, faculty expect students to provide more than technical correctness. They want students to achieve a balanced expertise, a balance that is between correctness and a knowledge set critical to effective written communication (or as an ESL professor notes, "You can't teach language without a content"). They report a concern that students need to understand and apply the requirements of particular written forms: the special demands of a nursing care plan, for example, or those of an academic essay or film review.

Yet, beyond even genre knowledge, these faculty insist that students demonstrate an understanding that probes and reflects and, in many cases, produces sound and productive actions. We've already seen how a math professor asks his students to demonstrate a metaknowledge of disciplinary learning. When it comes to care plans, nursing students, for example, need to demonstrate "that they are aware of clinical excellence, also a high standard of care . . . aware of patient safety issues, appropriate nursing actions." It became clear in the interviews that many, if not most of the faculty, want students to achieve a level of self-reflection that is deep indeed. A human services faculty member describes what he is after in a particular assignment involving a filmed interview of an agency volunteer:

> One of the things that I do in the interviewing class is at the end of the semester, maybe a week or two before the semester is over, they have a . . . published deadline to do an interview outside of class with a volunteer person. Somebody that is not part of this class, not part of this profession and above a certain age, [be]cause I don't want this to happen with kids. And they are playing the role of the helper or clinician and the other person is the client or whatever you want to call it. . . . And what they do is, it's just five minutes. It should have

a beginning, a middle, and an end, and I've given them all this information all along, and by the way, we've modeled this in class countless times by that point. . . . But what they have to do is they have to do this outside-of-class experience, submit the tape to me and only I see it, and they critique their own performance. And they're graded not on how well they performed on camera . . . but in recognizing their own good . . . practice and bad elements of practice and how they might do things differently and stuff. Very tremendously powerful assignment.

Similarly, a graphic design faculty member expects her students to describe the process by which they have created a project, taking care to express what worked, what didn't, and how they might have done things differently. Or take this assignment from an occupational therapy professor:

> I want students to become a little more comfortable with individuals with disabilities, and at the same time they need to be developing their listening skills and their communication skills and something called therapeutic uses, you know, talking to somebody and helping them be comfortable about sharing about themselves with you. So it's actually a very deep assignment, and the students, at the same time, are doing some reflection about how they're doing in terms of their communication skills. So they write about how the interview went. Then they have to think about what was it in what that person said that reflects the meaning of disability as we've talked about it, that reflects the meaning of occupation to an individual. How has their occupational performance, which is their ability to do things for themselves, been affected by their disability?

Later in the interview, the same faculty member poses these questions for her students, prompting them to achieve a feminist and postmodern perspective: "What aren't we hearing? What's not being said? What's missing here? . . . Who seems silenced? What are some of the politics behind some of this?"

PEDAGOGY: HELPING STUDENTS
REACH EXPECTATIONS

It is . . . appropriate to understand community colleges as
places where *multiple* standards operate simultaneously, reflecting the vast variety of students and their purposes. . . .
(Grubb 211)

Simplistic perceptions of the teaching and learning at community
colleges abound. Reductively, these notions go something like this:
as open admissions institutions and places of last resort, community
colleges receive students whose academic capabilities are limited.
Expectations, therefore, are severely cut back, with faculty opting to
"dumb down" their approaches in the classroom. In terms of writing
instruction, it would follow, therefore, that expectations would stall
at the editing and formal stages: faculty would place their focus on
academic forms such as the essay and would instruct mostly on ways
of editing work to insure sound grammar and mechanics. Students,
for their part, would expect to work within strict academic forms.
Moreover, given the heavy teaching load at our college, we wondered
whether faculty would have the time and energy to invest in promoting intensive writing instruction on campus. For example, would we
be likely to see faculty encouraging submission of multiple drafts for
teacher feedback? Would we be likely to see writing assigned outside
the usual general education courses such as English and history?
Would class and conference time be taken up with a discussion of
writing process? And would the writing tasks themselves challenge
both students and faculty alike?

Our study attempts to answer such questions and to document
teaching expectations and practices. In so doing we also want to
ascertain whether writing instruction at the college bears some relationship to its complex and comprehensive mission, namely, to
prepare students not only for successful transfer to four-year colleges
but also for smooth and effective transition into a career.

The results indicate the complex nature of writing instruction at
the college. Faculty recognize the vital importance of writing both
in the classroom and the work site, whether that site be the hospital

floor or the accounting cubicle. Particular value is placed on the technical correctness of writing, especially given the lack of a solid foundation in that area among so many of our students. But it is equally clear that faculty expect to build on that foundation, complementing a sound technical knowledge with a rhetorical awareness (of audience and purpose) and a sensitivity to the demands of genre (a review, an interview, a journal, a reflective self-critique).

TAKING A CLOSER LOOK AT THE ASSIGNMENTS

The approaches to teaching that seemed to have the most powerful effects on student writing . . . always had clear, specific objectives. Further, instructors appeared to have made objectives operationally clear to the students by modeling the procedures, coaching students through them in the early stages, or using specially designed activities to facilitate learning the new procedures. (Hillocks 58)

Occupational Therapy: The Reflective Interview Assignment

Community colleges are teaching-centered institutions whose mission is to prepare students not only for transfer to four-year institutions but also for careers in the workplace. Might not the writing assignments, then, that faculty use to engage students reveal both the careful scaffolding discussed by Hillocks and serve as a transition to the workplace?

Certainly that is the case when we examined closely an interview assignment given in a colleague's occupational therapy course. What is striking from the onset is the instructor's effort to make explicit the assignment's goals, phrased both in the language of the program and of academic convention. The teacher expected students to

- integrate relevant academic knowledge through case study;
- begin to develop the skills of self-awareness, listening, therapeutic communication, and interviewing;
- begin to understand how occupation and disability affect people and those around them;

- demonstrate basic computer competence by producing a word processed document; and
- use the APA format.

A connection is then made to the course content:

The assignment relates to the following course content: Occupational performance, the subjective meaning of occupation, the impact of disability on occupational performance and occupational role, therapeutic use of self, communication skills, and interview skills.

For this instructor, writing becomes an opportunity to engage students in the essential domain of the profession even as it prepares students for writing elsewhere in the academic curriculum. They are to demonstrate genuine therapeutic communication and listening skills even as they find their way to use word processing efficiently. They are to integrate knowledge gained from classroom discussion and readings with the facts of the case. In other words, students are encouraged to see knowledge as holistically constructed: this assignment is more than about using APA formatting properly but rather to use it in a way that serves the other goals of the assignment. This is more than an exercise in communicating skills but a use of those skills in the service of the "therapeutic self."

To assist students as they prepare for interviewing someone who has faced a "life challenge that resulted in a change in occupational performance," the instructor gives contact information for a community agency that will provide students with appropriate interview subjects. In addition, students are given "helpful hints," which are in part process-centered but also suggest some necessary content:

- Make an appointment and let the individual know that you are an occupational therapy assistant student who is just learning the profession.
- Pay attention to your feelings as you conduct the session.
- Begin with an assurance that all information is confidential.

- Share how the session will help you as a future practitioner. (This will reinforce the individual's sense of making a real contribution to you and the field.)
- End with a thank you.

We are struck with the modeling that is enacted in these suggestions, modeling, that is, of behaviors appropriate to the profession (keeping information about clients confidential, for example, or enabling the patient with a sense of how much she is teaching the reflective practitioner). The objective here is not to promote generic interview skills, although such can clearly be gleaned from this assignment (the teacher provides sample interview questions), but rather to embody such skills in the role of occupational therapist in training.

But the instructor endeavors to promote more than skills-based learning. She wants to enable a reflective practice by having students compose their professional selves through writing. Less concerned about genre ("Write a brief [3–4 pages] paper about the session"), the instructor enunciates a list of items and questions aimed at developing a metacognitive awareness and an emerging professional identity:

- Info on the individual's age, gender, socioeconomic, or cultural status that may influence his/her responses
- Occupational profile such as work history
- What is the primary problem, condition or diagnosis?
- What type of learning experience was this for you?
- What new insights have you gained?
- What new skills are you developing?
- What therapeutic communication strengths of your own did you draw on?
- What advice did the individual suggest to you that you think is important for your practice [as an occupational therapist] . . . ?

Students are encouraged not only to be "text processors" but "practitioners in training" (Walvoord and McCarthy 102). In other words, as the assignment clearly states, the instructor aims at teaching students not only "occupational performance and occupational role" but the critical nature and function of therapeutic communication. It is worth noting that in requiring students to think deeply about their own learning, the assignment fosters "reflection in action," making the clear statement that effective practice in the field must be accompanied by continuous reflection (Schön).

The instructor's evaluation rubric reveals in even more detail the hierarchy of concerns and expectations for students. In the matrix shown on the next page, goals are numbered as in the list above and apportioned by percentage and primary traits placed in one of three evaluative categories ("Exemplary," "Competent," and "Developing").

Knowledge sets directly related to the training of the professional in the field are given clear priority. Apparent as well is the instructor's segregating of "content" concerns and form, the latter of which includes the generalized and somewhat less valued (at 10 percent of the overall grade) category of "writing skills." The instructions jumble writing with technical skills such as word processing and use of the APA format. But even as we note the conventional dichotomy between form and content, we might take another look at the language used to describe the goals residing in the upper third of the rubric. The instructor expects students to "integrate" practical knowledge with "academic knowledge," to "understand" the impact of occupation and disability, and to "develop . . . self awareness [and] communication [skills]." Such integration and understanding are to be expressed necessarily in writing. In other words, while one might infer that writing is seen here as servicing such needs, it is just as reasonable to see writing as producing and constructing these higher-order outcomes.

The Visual Arts: Nature Close Up

This balance between preparing students to engage in the work of the profession and preparing them for the work of the academy is carefully preserved in an assignment for a course in visual arts. Introduced by Theodore Roethke's poem "Cuttings" ("One nub of growth / Nudges a sand crumb loose" [5–6]), the assignment begins by inviting students to observe nature "close up"—advising them to observe nature at the level of the grain of sand and microscopic cell

Goals	Exemplary
30% Integrate relevant knowledge about: occupational performance, subjective meaning of occupation, impact of disability on occupational performance and occupational role. Understand how occupation and disability affect people and those around them.	Thoughtfully comments on the interviewee's occupational performance, subjective meaning of occupation, impact of disability on occupational performance; and the impact of disability on occupational role. Includes all of Impact of age, gender, socioeconomic, or cultural status; Occupational Profile; and individual's response. Thoughtfully comments on how disability affects interviewee and those around him/her.
30% Develop the skills of self-awareness, listening, therapeutic communication and interviewing	Includes thoughtful comments on response to experience and type of learning experience, response to advice offered comments on new insights gained, comments on new skills developing. Notes strengths and areas to develop.
10% Basic computer competence	Paper is word processed document. . . .
10% Uses the APA format	Correct format for in-text citation and references
5% Maintains client confidentiality	No potentially identifiable info
5% Research and write paragraph on primary problem	Relevant. Paragraph in writer's words. Links researched info to interviewee's situation. Adequate length (min. 3 sentences).
10% Writing skills	Contains intro, body, and conclusion. Accurate grammar, punctuation and spelling. Interesting to read. Refrains from extraneous information. Stays within 3–4 page limit. Used [writing center] or [writing center]. Handouts. Includes title and 2 assessment forms.

Competent	Developing
Mentions all components but does not elaborate. Includes ⅔ of Impact of age, gender. . . . Mentions this but does not elaborate	Missing some components. Does not demonstrate understanding of the concepts Includes ⅓ of Impact of age, gender. . . . Does not mention how disability affects interviewee and those around him/her.
Mentions those areas but does not elaborate. Notes strengths or areas to develop.	Is missing components. Mentions some but does not elaborate. Does not note strengths or areas to develop.
Paper is word processed document . . . and contains some issues in use of fonts or formats	Paper is handwritten
Minor error in APA formatting. . . .	Two or more errors in APA formatting. . . .
1 or 2 compromise confidentiality	Confidentiality is violated
Relevant. Mainly direct quotes with minimal interpretation by student. Does not link to interviewee. 2 sentences.	Research is not relevant. All direct quotes with no interpretation by student. Does not link to interviewee. 1 sentence.
Contains intro, body, and conclusion. Minor errors in grammar, punctuation & spelling. Mostly interesting, bogs down in places. Minor extraneous information. Less than 3 or more than 4 pages. Used [writing center]. Is missing one component.	Contains intro. . . . Errors in grammar . . . distract and interfere with meaning. Difficult to read. A great deal of extraneous information. Less than 2 or more than 5 pages. Did not use [writing center]. Is missing two or more components.

but also at the level of local, requiring them to visit an art exhibit at the college:

> A close-up of nature can reveal a world that is usually over-looked by our more generalized or passing points of view. The ancient Roman philosopher Lucretius . . . was aware of the possibility of an atomic level to existence and our modern electron microscopes have shown us that his vision was both correct and intricately patterned. In the show "Lush," textile artists have presented us with their close-ups of our natural world. . . . Some of their interpretations are intricately pat-terned while others present detail asymmetrically and without regularized repetitions. Select two works, one patterned—one not, and after a brief description citing artist and material . . . compare the two, describing what in particular you think might have inspired the artists (plant growth, a stream bed, rainfall, ice . . .). Speculate on why the two artists might have arrived at such different views of nature close-up.

That poetry and visual art would be joined here is hardly sur-prising, but we may well note the injection of ancient philosophy (Lucretius) and modern electronoscopy. Clearly comfortable crossing disciplinary boundaries, the instructor invites her students to do the same—to the extent at least of considering connections between the poetic and visual, the imaginative and the scientific.

As with the assignment in occupational therapy, the writing is not genre specific but, instead, invites a comparison and contrast of the two art objects. Revealingly, the instructor invites students to "speculate" as to the reasons the two artists came to view nature so differently. Again, like her colleague in occupational therapy, the art instructor is mindful of process and the need to offer a scaffold or structure on which students can build their response. Students are to draw from a class reading before beginning to write their paper ("Responding to Art"). Appropriately, the next section of the assign-ment begins with "How to start?" What follows are developmentally sequenced procedures for accomplishing this assignment laid out in a template for note taking:

- Look around at the works. Choose two works, one patterned, and one not patterned.
- Work (patterned): Information about the work (artist and material, from the label).
- Sketch the work.

Students are then prompted to do the same for the second, non-patterned work. After such exposition, comparative analysis is set to begin:

- Compare the two works (jot down your notes now to help you in writing this paper later).
- What are the connections between the two works as well as distinctions between them?
- Describe in particular what may have inspired the artists.
- Speculate on why the two artists have arrived at such different views of nature.

The instructor urges students to "make sure your voice is clear in the paper—write in the first person (use 'I')." She continues, "We should be able to tell that these are your impressions or opinions. If you quote something from the description of the show, make sure you say something like 'According to the exhibit description. . . .'" Here the instructor sends the signal that the writer needs to be present in the writing while at the same time acknowledging the presence of others (the writing on the gallery wall). Source attribution is of course a key component of writing in the academy. The practice takes on added dimension in the visual arts, wherein intellectual property has a palpable quality. The art, comprised of physical materials and demonstrably installed before the viewer, demands to be recognized.

Yet the assignment calls for more than recognition of the art object. Students need to speculate as to the generative and imaginative processes that produced the object. Here the student must rely on the slender suggestions given earlier in the prompt ("plant growth," for example, as seen in the poem and referenced in the prompt). In addition, students must draw upon technical vocabulary as deployed in their textbook, *Visual Literacy: Writing about Art*. Both challenges represent tall orders for the novice student, no doubt. But it is worth noting that the objective, implicitly if not explicitly stated, is to achieve a kind of cross-border literacy: students must demonstrate competence with literacy, both visual and word-based, and must produce exposition, analysis, and speculation.

RESPONDING TO STUDENT WRITING

Writing pedagogy takes on an equally complex aspect with the faculty. Response becomes key. Taking a look at the feedback offered to students in the cohort studied, a limited sample, faculty do seem to engage in dialogue with students, helping to prepare them for the work of the academy, although at times the comments ask and answer a question as opposed to encouraging students to process and respond in a subsequent draft.

Though the faculty surveyed report that they expect more than technical correctness, those in this nonrepresentative sample do seem to comment most frequently upon issues of technical correctness. Each has a system of doing so and focuses on a particular set of errors. It is common for each instance of a particular error to be identified throughout a draft. Many are directive, making changes in punctuation, spelling, grammar, and phrasing for students, both on drafts in progress and final drafts. When students have multiple writing assignments in a single course, the method of feedback generally does not vary across assignments.

A number of instructors do attempt to point out areas of drafts that are successful, though the reasons for such a reaction are not always revealed. At other times, the positive feedback doesn't obviously coincide with the assignment guidelines. One set of responses to a student's essay exam in a study skills course, for example, focused primarily on the effective use of humor in response to the following directive: "Select one learning strategy from the book that helped you with your classes and explain how it helped."

Another recurring practice of faculty, in this particular sample, is circling or otherwise drawing attention to certain areas of the text. At times these sections are annotated, but at times there isn't an indication as to why these sections are highlighted. This occurs at the word, sentence, and paragraph level.

While a number of faculty comment extensively on student work, some drafts include only a note at the end of the paper (for example, "Good Job"). In-text and marginal comments are less frequent for papers written in subjects other than English, though faculty in these disciplines do offer feedback across the range mentioned. Some left checkmarks at various spots in the paper with no written explanation while others asked students probing questions and engaged with the subject matter of the paper. A chemistry professor, for instance, responded to a lab report in which the student had investigated the density of a solid piece of copper: "Quite high error. Are you sure you used copper?" A student in a general psychology course reflected in a journal entry about coping with the stress she felt as a college student: "I want to just sit down or quit and say forget about it." The instructor responded: "Tina—We have a lot of great and helpful people here at BCC who would be very interested in getting you connected with a counselor. I'd be very willing and eager to bring you over to the counseling department and help you make an appointment there."

With only a couple of exceptions, when drafts were involved, instructors reviewed an early draft and a final draft. Generally, both were graded, with the final draft having a higher grade assigned. At times this new grade is "predicted" through end comments such as "A-. Revise for an A." Drafts were far more likely to have been reviewed by the instructor, and commented upon, in English courses.

We realize that the assignments discussed here cannot and should not reveal the nature and extent of the writing assignments required by all faculty nor, indeed, can these 70-plus, mostly full-time faculty whom we surveyed and interviewed speak for the 477 full- and part-time faculty and staff who work at the college. Nevertheless, we hope that we have begun to dislodge some simplistic notions of community college writing instruction. Not all assignments are merely "skill and drill" in nature. Nor do they all call for summaries or, as our students, fresh from high school, refer to them, "reports." Instead, faculty challenge students to reflect deeply on the problems before them, problems typically tied to the working world that they will soon enter but firmly rooted in academic convention.

4

Student Expectations and Practices

WHEN BEN, ONE OF our cohort of students, revealed to us that in addition to taking a full course load of classes (four courses) at night, he held two jobs (at a coffee shop and a radio station) working roughly forty hours a week, we were hardly surprised. After all, we had learned anecdotally from our own students that it had become the norm to work at least twenty hours while taking a full-time course load. Studies of other colleges painted the same picture. The recent Study of Entering Student Engagement, for example, published in its preliminary findings that 47 percent of its pilot respondents reported working more than twenty hours a week ("Starting Right"). In the late 1990s, the National Center for Education produced even more startling statistics when it reported that over 80 percent of community college students were working either full or part time (with about 50 percent of those working full time ("Employment Status"). What we had not sufficiently understood until speaking to students like Ben was that he and the others want little in the way of concessions for their hectic school and work loads. Instead, what we heard from him and others is the need to be treated like an adult, someone who, even at the tender age of eighteen (as Ben is), has considerable maturity. Show us what it takes to succeed, they say, and we will take it from there.

Our students, and community college students generally, are not unique in facing the twin demands of college and work: 82 percent of all college students have jobs outside of college, with 32 percent working full-time jobs (Donoghue 90). But studies always show that community college students tend to be older, are more likely to be the first in their family to go to college, and more likely to be enrolled in at least one developmental course than their counterparts at four-year institutions (Bailey and Davis Jenkins 8, 18, 25). According to the Two-Year College English Association's "Two-Year College Facts and Data Report" of 2005, 73 percent of two-year college students were nontraditional, meaning that they had at least one of the following characteristics: delayed enrollment into college after high school, attended part time, worked full time, were financially independent for financial aid purposes, had dependents other than a spouse, were single parents, or did not have a high school diploma or equivalent ("Two-Year College Student Body Profile"). Persisting amid such formidable challenges became a leitmotif for our students. Some found support from family; others needed to look elsewhere: to mentors, friends, and college staff. Many managed to derive an inner strength—in part fueled by a desire to achieve despite all the odds.

In our study we focused on a student population that hadn't yet been influenced by college instruction, new college students with untested expectations, perceptions, and attitudes. Our original cohort consisted of sixteen students, all but two of whom were female, their ages ranging from eighteen to thirty-five. Eleven enrolled as full-time students (twelve credits). Students' concentrations varied: six were business majors, three liberal arts, two health science, one elementary education, one early childhood education, one communication, one criminal justice, and one student had not declared a major program of study. Eight took at least one remedial course.

A SURVEY OF STUDENT ATTITUDES AND PRACTICES AS WRITERS

To lay a foundation for our study and to provide much needed context against which to read cohort writing, we gathered information about student attitudes toward writing and about their writing practices through surveys. A survey was administered to first-time students at four two-year colleges from different regions of the country, including our own, Bristol. As mentioned earlier, while our focus was on the local population at Bristol, we sought to ascertain whether Bristol students responded in a manner consistent with other two-year college students. New first-semester students were surveyed at Bristol Community College, Santa Barbara City College, Illinois Central College, and Whatcom Community College. In total, over 1,350 surveys were collected.

The survey aimed to ascertain a range of student perceptions but emphasized three in particular: students' attitudes about writing in general, perceptions of their own writing processes, and experiences in high school relative to writing instruction. We hoped to gain a better idea of student writing behaviors as well as what they'd learned about the nature of writing. We also hoped, and were pleased to note, that Bristol's students were comparable to their counterparts in the targeted colleges for all three areas.

Cohort students were also surveyed and the results compared to surveys administered to non-cohort Bristol students. Results indicate that cohort students felt more confident as writers than non-cohort students. Cohort students, not surprisingly then, looked forward in greater numbers to challenging writing assignments and would be more likely than non-cohort students to seek out courses that require writing. Cohort students also reported less experience than non-cohort Bristol students with working in groups while in high school. That fact may explain the independence displayed by many of our cohort students. As so many shuttle from work to class and back, working well on one's own would seem to be an advantage.

Of the students surveyed at Bristol, Santa Barbara, Illinois Central, and Whatcom, 90 percent expected to write regularly in college. Only about a third of students surveyed considered themselves strong writers (and just 28 percent of the students at Bristol), suggesting they may have had some less-than-affirming experiences with writing in the past. Despite their lack of confidence, students were hopeful that improvement was possible, as 84 percent thought they could develop their writing skills. What we didn't ask is what students thought would need to happen in order for that improvement to occur.

While nearly all, 95 percent, of respondents thought that writing was an important skill for college students, many considered writing a temporary evil; about half, 48 percent, didn't think writing would be important in their chosen careers. Nearly all faculty, a solid 95 percent, thought writing would be important in those same fields. Clearly faculty will need to do some persuading here, although it makes sense that students wouldn't have made firm career choices by this point, much less thoroughly investigated the duties and responsibilities involved.

Do students actively seek to develop their writing skills? While a significant majority of survey respondents thought it was possible, only 19 percent reported actually seeking out courses that required writing. On the other hand, they didn't seem to avoid writing intensive courses either, despite 58 percent of Bristol faculty believing they did so, with only 9 percent of the students admitting to avoidance. About 26 percent of respondents indicated that they look forward to challenging writing assignments. It seems that, while 84 percent of students thought they could develop their writing skills, a smaller number was actually eager to do so.

Fifty-eight percent thought their high school writing instruction had prepared them to write papers in college. This feeling of readiness was dependent on whether they'd done work in groups (N = 710, p < .001), written research papers (N = 824, p < .001), and used classmates' feedback to revise drafts (N = 768, p < .001) while in high school. There were also strong correlations among involvement in these activities and students' feeling confident about their writing skills. Despite 58 percent of respondents' feeling prepared for the demands of college writing, only 34 percent believed the writing they would do in college would be similar to what they'd done in high school. These figures suggest students may not anticipate any difference between high school and college writing—or any elevation in challenge.

Several questions asked students to think about teacher feedback on their writing in high school. A solid 94 percent reported finding the feedback to be helpful. Interestingly, just 24 percent thought that such assessments of their writing matched their own. This might suggest, in combination with the previous response, that students are (perhaps too) open to others' suggestions for improvement. Most students, 84 percent, were used to receiving both negative and positive feedback, so it is logical that they would expect both in college.

Questions that investigated students' writing processes revealed some areas where faculty perceptions and student behaviors conflicted. For example, though only 6 percent of faculty thought that students began papers when assigned, 45 percent of the students reported doing so—at least in the past. Although only 13 percent of Bristol's faculty thought students were used to producing multiple drafts of their work, approximately 57 percent of students claimed to do so.

Students revealed that they engaged in some activities that faculty thought were beneficial, including coming up with ideas before writing, a task 76 percent of respondents engaged in, and rereading papers before handing them in, a practice of 85 percent of students surveyed. Revision, particularly that which responds to reader feedback, wasn't practiced by all respondents; 46 percent reported showing their writing to someone before handing it in—this despite having experience with drafting and feedback in high school: 60 percent had experience with peer review and about 73 percent had to revise papers using teacher feedback. It would seem reasonable for students to expect to have to engage in similar practices in college. Finally, most students, 79 percent, had written a paper using research while in high school.

HOW MUCH WRITING AND WHAT KINDS?

When we asked students to collect all the writing that they had done in the fall of 2007, we were under no illusions as to the challenges. We knew that students at the college lived hectic lives and that committing themselves to bringing written work to our office routinely would be a tall order. And so it was. Some work was handed in missing pages; other work was promised but not handed in at all. Nevertheless, we received from our cohort of sixteen nearly 120 pieces of writing, not including class notes. In many cases, multiple drafts of particular projects were submitted, together with faculty commentary and grades.

An overwhelming predominance of writing—roughly 80 percent—came from English courses, either developmental writing or the required composition course. Did this surprise us? Not really, because the assumption among faculty and new students is that the required writing course or, in the case of a failed placement test, a basic writing course would provide the basis for most of the writing during the first semester. Roughly 30 percent of the writing drew from external sources (print or visual). Over two-thirds of that writing was assigned in students' English courses. Thus, we concluded that few opportunities to write were given in other courses and that relatively little attention was paid in English, or any other course, to writing with sources—presumably a representative form of college-level writing.

Written genres ran the gamut. Most typical was the essay, with current traditional emphases on definition, classification or division, narrative, description, and process. The reliance on conventional modes of expository prose confirms what Grubb has characterized as skills-based instruction routinely provided at community colleges (Grubb 28). Still, a more complex picture of writing instruction emerges from the remaining genres represented in student portfolios: the memoir, film review, peer review, experimental lab report, journal (especially informal reactions to reading), writer's autobiography, resume and cover letter. Such general categories say little, of course, about how students met the challenges posed by each opportunity to write. To gauge student performance in detail, we needed to study cases of individual students.

TINA: THINKING CATEGORICALLY

Nineteen years of age in the fall of 2007, Tina was the first in her family to have graduated from high school or vocational school, and the first to attend college full time (her sister had attended night school for a time). An elementary education major, Tina had set her sights on becoming an elementary school teacher since she herself attended grammar school. Tina had expressed to us how much she enjoyed being with young children. She had volunteered a good deal of her time as a classroom aide and had volunteered in the community since middle school.

As a full-time student, Tina took four courses in the fall of 2007: basic writing, the West and the World (history), general psychology, and College Reading and Learning Strategies. She earned a 3.67 grade point average despite reporting to be "overwhelmed" by the work. Tina in many respects is typical of our students in that she was required to take developmental courses, in her case, writing and reading. Not surprisingly, Tina expressed considerable frustration with the amount and difficulty of the reading. Reflecting on her first semester in an assignment offering advice to new students to the college, Tina wrote, "You may want to pick up your speed on your reading . . . in Psychology, I have to read sometimes a chapter or two a night [as she did in high school] but all of the chapters have about seven to eight modules in each which are extensive." Elsewhere she writes, "I have never had to read so much before ever. I never have liked reading unless it is reading in a group . . . the only reading I ever did was what I had to. I never read for 'fun' as many people do. I do wish I could do that and enjoy doing so, but I still am working on it. This has also been a struggle at home because neither my [sic] parents can read very well or even understand some of the things we get to do."

Tina is in some respects a familiar story at our college: a first-generation college student for whom the jump from high school to college is challenging. With little in the way of academic support at home, she must find that support elsewhere. Tina made considerable use of the college's academic support services, including the college's writing center, where she visited often and routinely. By her own admission an A student in her vocational high school, Tina discovered that what worked there doesn't seem to work at college: "I was still used to the 'high school method.' That is, you get an assignment to do, do it, pass it in for a grade, and if you're not satisfied with your grade you can revise it one time to get a higher grade."

In contrast, Tina discovered, college faculty, at least in her first semester, require lots of writing: "I have writing to do every single night and I have writing in psychology, writing in English, writing in reading, writing in history. I'm taking four courses, so I have writing in all of it . . . notes from the book and definitions, key terms. . . ." And plenty of rewriting, too: "Here it's just rewriting and rewriting and rewriting, and sometimes I don't know if I'm writing it good enough or if I'm not including enough detail because there's not enough information on the paper. . . . I have like six drafts for each piece of writing I've done. . . . Whenever I was in high school—that's all I can compare to—is you do your first draft, you do your corrections, you do your second draft—that's your final draft."

Admittedly accustomed to, and dependent on, the "red ink" of teachers' responses to her high school writing, Tina reported feeling uncomfortable with the independence that college instructors expect her to exhibit as a writer: "sometimes it seems like I'm putting the same information together because I don't know what else to add, or I don't know what to take out, and I like to keep everything all together that I write. I don't like taking things out."

In short, Tina, whose past practice as a student involved collecting and organizing all her work, suddenly found herself with so much written work, including multiple drafts for each assignment, that she struggled with information overload. Her work with tutors at the writing center—including with us—suggested a need to be directed to the correct path to take, even as writing center practice and theory rests fundamentally on the need to nurture writers' independence. A similar dissonance occurred in her college work generally as instructors expect her and other students to demonstrate critical thinking and writing skills and a self-monitoring of their own writing practices—challenges for which Tina felt unprepared. All that said, we note with assurance Tina's ability to perform well in her classes, as her writing portfolio and grades attest.

As we reviewed her portfolio, we confirmed that the first semester of college brought plenty of writing opportunities. In basic writing, we saw multiple drafts of twelve papers (the first one of which, a process paragraph, begins with the telling statement, "I Don't Hate Writing"). In general psychology, we saw extended journal entries for each of twelve chapters of the class textbook as well as two formal essays in various drafting stages. In the West and the World, we noted half a dozen quizzes, exams, and worksheets. In reading, Tina included class notes and worksheets. It is important to emphasize that what we saw in the portfolio is what Tina brought to us—which applies to the portfolios of all the cohort. Given Tina's admitted habit of collecting everything—including drafts—we feel confident that we have an accurate representation of her writing in this first semester of college. Most of the writing collected came from the English and psychology courses.

For her first formal writing assignment in English, Tina was challenged to achieve a level of metacognition that characterizes college-level work: "I'd like you to explain your writing process," asks her instructor. "You'll want to refer to, in sufficient detail, particular essays, reports, letters, and other documents you've written." In so requesting, the instructor sends the message that writing encompasses more than the school-sanctioned genre of the essay.

The assignment calls for a "process paragraph." However, Tina made it clear early on that she wanted to extend her thinking beyond a single paragraph. We reproduce what appears to be the first draft that receives teacher commentary:

> I don't hate writing and I don't love writing. It's a "love-hate relationship." If I had to write about community help, children or the elderly, writing would come easily to me because I have had the experience with helping out in the community, also with children and the elderly. I can write about these subjects because I've participated with them all.

> Writing comes hard to me when I do not like the subject or topic. I get frustrated and want to say "forget about it" and just go out to a place to let my frustration out. Also if I have no way of getting around, I will just go in my room and listen to music. That is what I usually go and do. All of this pertains to my writing process.

Tina, like many a naïve writer, expresses a desire to write about what she "like[s]." For Tina, that would mean writing about her

community service, an area to which she is profoundly committed. What she likes amounts, then, to what she knows, which in
turn translates into a fluency. While it is tempting to dismiss Tina's
need to write about what she likes as an evasion of the hard work of
college-level writing, perhaps we need to put ourselves into Tina's
position. In doing so, we might see that she has just begun a journey
to discover not just what she likes to write about but what she can
write about. In other words, her journey is one of discovering her
own competency and capability.

Tina's instructor, in his commentary, asked to know more about
the difficult topics to which the paper alludes. Presumably, in confronting such topics from the past, Tina would begin the process of
learning through difficulty. Her revisions, however, proved evasive.
Instead of providing information on a specific course or actual topic
about which she had written, Tina asserted, "Any topic could really
fit." Growing more frustrated, the instructor was not given what
he sought: more detailed information as to topics she found challenging in the past. "I've suggested focusing solely on the issue of
topic selection," he writes, "if you decide to revise further," noting,
however, the useful information provided about her writing practice
and history.

A similar disconnect occurred when Tina was asked by her instructor to "write about a subject with which you are quite familiar."
Now, this subject would seem to be the answer to Tina's prayers,
in the light of what she noted in the paper just discussed. But the
instructor was after something more than a mere description of what
Tina knows: "This assignment gives you lots of freedom, so we do
need to establish some parameters. The goal of this assignment is to
write with a *purpose* in mind. You'll be discussing a familiar topic
to achieve a particular end. In other words, you may write about a
serious car accident to convey the importance of buckling up. . . .
What I want you to keep in mind is what readers will learn—how
they will benefit—from reading your paper."

Tina's essay, titled "Why Become a Volunteer with Children?"
underwent several drafts. Taken together, the versions show Tina
attempting to bring a description of her community service in line

with the purpose of the essay (expressed in the title and required by the assignment): to persuade the reader to consider community service. An early draft focused explicitly on Tina's early experience volunteering:

> Beginning in elementary school . . . , I helped with children that had disabilities both mental and physical. That was a new field for me and I also loved it. It took a lot more effort but it was all worth it.

> Also I was President of the Key Club. . . . We helped with children. . . .

In a later draft, labeled by Tina "Revision 5," she added material noting teachers to whom Tina went for help while she was in elementary school, teachers who provided "modeling techniques." Her instructor commented, not surprisingly, "Unclear how this relates to thesis." Tina's working thesis throughout her many drafts (by the count given in the portfolio, there were six) was "In my volunteering experience with children, I have learned a variety of things about myself and the children I work with." Tina was determined to tell the story of her coming to volunteer work, despite the expectation that her writing provide explicit direction to a reader (her instructor writes, "Thesis is clear, but will readers benefit?"). Interestingly, when she did write about the benefits of volunteering, Tina focused on the benefits to herself: "A personal advantage of volunteering for me has been learning about myself. To name some experience, I have learned to control my temper, I've become more patient, I have become more professional and I also see myself as more of an adult."

What is happening here, exactly? Why did Tina have difficulty staying on task? And is there a connection between her challenge in this paper and the struggle expressed in the earlier assignment to relay specific, pertinent information about topics of difficult writing assignments? We surmise that Tina, in the educational theorist Robert Kegan's terms, was being challenged to move from "categorical thinking" to the higher principle of "cross-categorical knowing" (26). Imagine, Kegan writes, the struggles of an adolescent to communicate his desire for independence (being out past curfew) with his parents' set of expectations for what that means to them (establishing limits): "In order for him [Matty, the adolescent] actually to hold their point of view in a way in which he could identify with it, he would have to give up an ultimate or absolute relationship to his own point of view" (24).

Kegan posits that giving up an "absolute relationship to his own point of view" is a necessary step to recognizing a mutual relationship between one's own point of view and the view of others. One must continually cross back and forth between such categories. But Kegan goes further with important implications for educators: This third level of consciousness, as Kegan sees it, is a prerequisite for the ability to shuttle between different planes of knowing—between, for example, the concrete and the abstract, between an awareness of what we want to say and an awareness of how we say it and why. This level of thinking, a higher order of consciousness, characterizes much college-level work and demands that instructors create bridges to allow students to move from the second to the third level. Returning to Tina: her struggle to understand fully the demands of her reader (the instructor) is but one piece of evidence suggesting that she, at this point of our reading of her work, is in Kegan's "second-level of consciousness," defined by "durable categories." Other evidence might include her difficulty as she grapples to articulate the purpose of her writing beyond providing evidence for a grade (for example, writing in order to assist someone to enter into community service or writing that recalls topics that have been difficult to engage in the past and reflection on the reasons for such difficulty). Yet, in her determination to receive feedback to her writing—as demonstrated in the sheer number of drafts submitted for review by teachers and tutors—Tina expresses a desire to have a meeting of minds, as it were, with her readers and thereby lay the groundwork for a higher-order thinking

Fortunately for Tina, much of the writing asked of her in her general psychology course entailed a reflection of her learning behavior and thus promoted the kind of introspection that will be expected in courses to come.

In one assignment, Tina needed to write an essay describing how her "understanding of memory has changed as a result of reading and thinking" about a chapter from her textbook. Students were urged to select topics "that are most relevant to your own improvement." In other words, the instructor saw this assignment as providing students with the means of altering their own behavior (for "improvement"). That was a timely message for Tina, who confided that often she cannot recall what she has read, due to an unnamed disability. In addition, the assignment, in calling for the use of at least one scholarly article, begins the process of inserting Tina into academic conversations within the field of general psychology—and in the process making her aware that her own point of view is not absolute.

Yet blurriness of focus and an inability to "cross categories" remained problems for Tina, as we see in this passage from her paper on memory:

> I learned that the hippocampus is a part of the brain that relates to emotion and the transferring of information from short-term memory to long-term. I am most familiar with short-term memory because I never remember details for very long. I have tried many aids to help my memory, but nothing seems to work. For example, when going over my work, I forget everything immediately. Another example that prevents me from maintaining information is stress-related. Stress prevents me from remembering information. I have a major problem with encoding because I have difficulty grasping information in large amounts. I can comprehend material in smaller amounts.

Again viewing the reading through the lens of her own experience, Tina gave little evidence of entering into the material that she gleaned from the reading. Seemingly ignoring the connection established in her opening sentence between emotion and the transferral of information from short- to long-term memory, Tina insisted on discussing her struggles to remember what she reads without any mention of emotion. While prompted to recall the subject of memory, she would rather detail not her short-term memory but her lack of memory at all. But then she felt it necessary to raise the matter of stress before she returned to her problem with "encoding." Of course, the subject of stress might very well be relevant to the initial observation that emotion can affect memory. But Tina was unable to make the connection convincingly in the writing. A wall has been constructed between what she had read and what she experiences—recalling Kegan's "durable category," more precisely, the limits of one's own perspective (25). Tina listed what she gleaned from the reading without making it her own. Poignantly, Tina was caught between a desire ("I want to achieve an active memory") and a reality ("I have read the entire chapter and tried some of the strategies, but still none have seemed to work for me"). "What we want," writes Kegan on behalf of the parents of adolescents, "is a single thing: a qualitatively new way of making sense, a change of mind as dramatic as the change a child undergoes between the ages of five and ten" (28). We believe that Tina's instructors and tutors wish the same for Tina: that she achieve a kind of "mutuality," an ability to associate the values of others with her own ideals (Kegan 35). By semester's end, Tina had not reached that result.

KIM: OWNING THE WRITING

Kim, age thirty-five in the fall of 2007 when our study began, was a liberal arts major who at that time had no declared concentration. She lives locally with her husband and her daughter. In her first semester at the college, Kim enrolled in six courses (a full-time load would be four courses), completed all six and earned a grade point average of 3.8 (including a basic writing course that that she elected to take the summer before). She has a full-time job during the day (she schedules her classes in evenings and weekends to accommodate the demands of work and family) at a multinational, full-service mortgage finance company. When contemplating a return to school after many years, a friend who happened to work at the local community college suggested she enroll there. Not certain how she would fare after being out of school for almost two decades, Kim decided to take a single course, Basic Writing, which she took in the summer to build her confidence. She described the rationale for placing herself in a developmental writing course in this way: it's "like a pair of shoes you try on before you run." While her husband was supportive of her decision to return to school, her parents were less so, claiming that she's "too old to go to school" and that it won't help her "make more money."

That lack of encouragement and the sheer time that had elapsed since leaving school prompted Kim to doubt her abilities as a writer. "I wasn't sure until recently that I possessed any ability to write whatsoever," she confided. Given her lack of confidence, Kim claimed to avoid writing but, in fact, she does a good deal of it at her day job: "proposals . . . team development projects . . . subordinate reviews . . . peer reviews, emails, project reports." Despite her lack of confidence as a writer, it became clear that Kim could speak with knowledge and authority when discussing the various demands posed by writing challenges in her first semester. For example, when describing, early in the semester, what she considered "the best paper" she's written, a lab report for biology, Kim confidently ticked off the requirements of that genre: "I was able to take the information from the data that we collected, report on it, assess it, and project a feasible outcome in the future or make a future prediction based off of that. I think it was a compilation of taking the data and then applying it . . . the data was solid . . . it had clear structure and focus." Kim was equally articulate during a second interview, occurring deep into her first semester, when she discussed what it takes to write well in history (she was taking both parts of a two-semester U.S. history course at once): "all our tests, quizzes on a weekly basis have all been in essay format which is kind of neat because he stays on persuasion in your writing . . . you have to pick a side and you have to able [*sic*] to support it, so I've done more working on developing thesis statements in my history class than I have in any other class."

A review of her portfolio suggested that opportunities for persuasive writing were not uniformly offered throughout Kim's classes. In her required college writing course, for example, the emphasis was on narration ("Write on a 'character' who goes 'against the tide' or on a 'defining moment' in one's life") or definition ("Define the word 'kindness' and what it *personally* means to you"). The instructor's prompts encouraged Kim to stay in the narrative and experiential mode rather than in the argumentative. Nevertheless, Kim appeared ready to take on additional challenges as a writer. In her second interview, Kim expressed much more confidence in her writing abilities: "I recognize that I control my writing. I have the power to control my thought process. I have the power to deliver a message, to communicate it effectively . . . it enables me to make those riskier decisions or what may have been riskier to me before but are now obvious."

Her confidence spilled over into interactions with her professors. Recalling a conversation that she had with her English professor, who claimed that "to get an A, you would have to write a perfect paper," Kim responded, "That's absolutely fine. And you need to define what a perfect paper would be in English 11 [our required, first semester writing course]." Kim added, "She didn't. She didn't have the ability to define what a perfect paper in English 11 would be." Concluding, Kim reflected on what she had learned about the "relationship between the paper and the feedback": "Whereas before I would look to my teacher to give me ideas as to where to go on my paper, now I think what I'm thinking for is to let me know what the parameters are for my paper. Rather than where should I be doing, set the limitations as to where you want what's expected."

Kim seemed to be saying that she was ready to take ownership of her writing while respecting the expectations of her reader. Indeed, Kim extended the concept of ownership to her education generally: "I think part of that is ownership in my education. I think part of that is ownership in the work that I've produced because it belongs to me. So I was having this conversation . . . with my biology teacher the other day because I . . . was saying, 'What were your office hours,' and she said, 'They're by appointment,' and I said, 'That's great. Let's make one because this, this is mine. I own this.'"

This newfound confidence led Kim understandably to express disappointment in her English course because she felt the instructor was narrow in her focus, quizzing students weekly on spelling words "like 'lead' or 'led.'" This seemed like a reprise of high school, where the focus had been much narrower, forcing Kim to think more about presentation than content. Fortunately, Kim has now been exposed to writing in a variety of settings expressing a variety of functions. In college, she can stretch and grow. She is ready to do so.

Kim's portfolio from the fall 2007 semester contained writing from four of her six classes: U.S. history, general psychology, biology, and College Writing. By far, the most writing came from the English course, for which Kim wrote seven reaction papers and three essays. Four of the pieces included at least one revision. The teacher's comments were interspersed throughout the collection. From U.S. history, we were given an informational research paper—apparently a final draft but with no sign of teacher commentary. From general psychology, we were shown an autobiography with apparent application of psychological theory, as a rough draft, with the writer's own comments included. We did not get a final version of the autobiography. In contrast with the formally academic writing in her other courses, the biology entry consisted of a desktop-published newsletter and brochure (on red tides).

As noted earlier, Kim's writing for her College Writing course, a course required of all students in all programs, emphasizes narration and definition, although it does include writing in the form of brief responses to selected readings. In reading her portfolio, we found two developments especially interesting: (a) Kim's revisions when responding to teacher commentary and (b) the qualitative difference between her expository writing (narration/definition) and her critical writing (reactions to reading).

An early assignment required Kim to write a narrative on a "defining moment" in her life. The paper begins, unexpectedly, with a strange joining of two important facets in Kim's life: family and a philosophy of doing "what needed to be done": "I have a daughter who is becoming a self-assured young person, a marriage based upon mutual respect, and a comfortable home. I love and admire my family and they do me as well. I got lucky! I'll say it again, 'I got lucky'; because every decision I've made for the past sixteen years was based upon a miss-guided [sic], ill-informed concept of, 'What needed to be done' as a parent."

Each stage in her family's life presents a new challenge: the birth of her daughter, Stephanie, when Kim was nineteen; shuttling Stephanie from horseback riding to guitar lessons to lacrosse games to cheer-leading practice; the decision to marry her husband Ed; working two full-time jobs while buying their first home. Each challenge is met with firm resolve rooted in the principle of doing "what needed to be done." Each paragraph, marking a life stage, concludes with that expression. Moreover, Kim is surprisingly candid when recounting these events as this account describing her motivation to marry can attest: "I married him because he was the father of my child, and the person I shared a home with. Getting married seemed like a must, in order to provide structure and stability. I never thought about the rest of my life or his. Truth be told getting married was just part of, 'What needed to be done.' Fortunately for both Ed and I [sic], we love and respect each other, a happy coincidence."

We still haven't learned what the "defining moment" in Kim's life is, although any of these landmarks seem likely candidates. A predictable paper might have provided Stephanie's birth as just that moment, or the day that Kim and Ed got married. But this is not a conventional paper, nor is Kim a conventional writer. She has decided to present that moment at the very end of the paper and as a deeply ironic moment in her life:

I am proud to boast that Stephanie is growing into a caring sensitive young person. She is an honor student, 3 sport athlete and volunteers time with local charities. Last May she came home from school and informed me that she would be spending the summer on the continent of Africa. I chuckled and asked, "Oh really why? [sic] She responded with, "There are tons of children dying or orphaned by AIDS over there and something [sic] should care enough to do something." I told her that I agree and understand but didn't think it was a good idea, to which she responded, "Mom, of all people you should know, sometimes you need to do what needs to be done."

I was horror-stricken of her going through life just doing, "What needs to be done." It's sad to say but it took those words emanating from my daughter's mouth to bring clarity to my life. Finally I realized that, I forced my daughter through countless hours of activities, worked myself to the point of exhaustion, and married a man for all the wrong reasons. I had spent her entire life modeling that, feelings, [*sic*] and physical well being were secondary to task completion. She had shown me that sometimes, "What needs to be done," should be done because someone cares enough to do it.

Kim took a gamble here, a gamble that doesn't quite pay off. She waited until the very end to establish the "defining moment," that experience when, according to her teacher's instructions, "you can go one way or the other." Kim may have intended to build to a climax or to surprise her reader dramatically at the end, but in practice the strategy did not work, at least at this stage in the drafting process. Detecting the problem, Kim's teacher commented in response to the paper's last sentence: "doesn't that also apply to why you did what you did?" In other words, it is unclear, on the basis of the last sentence, how Stephanie's plan is any different from the direction that Kim's life has taken to this point: they both are guided by "what needed to be done." Kim wanted to distinguish her daughter's perspective from her own but couldn't bring it off—at least not yet. She made adjustments, however, when she revised her draft. We replicated the original and tracked the changes that Kim made to her concluding paragraph:

> The words fell upon me like a ton of bricks. I was horror-stricken of her going through life just doing, "What needs to be done." I realized that I had been so busy pushing through life to get things done I forgot to enjoy it. It's sad to say but it took those words emanating from my daughter's mouth to ~~bring clarity to my life~~ make me evaluate my choices. Finally I realized that, I forced my daughter through countless hours of activities, worked myself to the point of exhaustion, and married a man for all the wrong reasons. I had spent her entire life modeling that, feelings, and physical well being were secondary to task completion. ~~She had shown me that sometimes, "What needs to be done," should be done because someone cares enough to do it.~~ Now instead of spending every day focused on task completion I take time to enjoy life. I guess that's "what needs to be done" now.

It's an imperfect closing, still, in that Kim does not provide an answer to her daughter's query. Indeed, Kim seems to set up a parallel between her daughter's philanthropic motives and her own admittedly self-centered pragmatism. Finally, Kim does not provide any evidence of acting on the change in her life, merely asserting a change. Nevertheless, Kim is clearly aware of the problem in the paragraph and has moved to clarify matters in response to the dissonance experienced by her instructor/reader.

After this revision, Kim's instructor asked two additional content-based questions. In the paragraph describing Kim's vow to do what was necessary to raise her newborn, the instructor asks, "Where was your support system?" Later, in response to the account of Kim's marriage when Stephanie was six, the instructor wonders about her husband, "Was he part of her life earlier?" Both questions show the instructor using a reader-based perspective, sensing a gap that needs to be filled. Kim, in revising her draft, chose to oblige her reader on these two points. In addition, her instructor circled the repeated use of the word "I" in her earlier draft. Kim made an effort here, too, but naturally comes up against the problem of needing to retain a prominent presence as "I" in a personal narrative. Nevertheless, Kim made some conscious stylistic choices, including subordination of phrases, to meet the instructor halfway. We again reproduce the pertinent passages and track the changes that Kim made:

> Giving birth at nineteen, ~~I was nineteen when I gave birth to~~ ~~my daughter Stephanie. I was young~~ insecure and terrified. The only person more frightened than I was the baby's father, Ed. ~~I remember feeling as though I was watching my life from~~ ~~a dream.~~ The first time the D~~octor~~. placed her in my arms I remember thinking that "I would do whatever I needed to take care of her." The only problem was that I had no idea what was needed. In the delivery room Ed looked at me and said, "Kim, you need to tell me what to do because I'm lost. My mother had took [*sic*] one look at Stephanie and announced, "She makes me feel old, I'm done with being a grandmother," with that she exited the room and the next three years of our

lives. My father was on wife number three (in five years) and not much assistance either. Despite my lack of direction, I vowed I would do, "What needed to be done no matter what." Reading I started reading the pamphlets the hospital provided, I and decided the core necessities were attention and education, stability, and a loving family.

Somewhat perplexingly, the instructor's final comments did not reference any criteria implicit in the instructions but, after noting the "great potential" of the paper and the need to "tighten the overall editing," offered only this content-based observation: "I think you are a little hard on yourself." Clearly, Kim demonstrated a willingness to "do what is needed" to meet her instructor's demands, unclear though they were.

Kim's responses to the class readings provided a counterpoint to the mostly expository work of her formal writing. In these brief reaction papers, Kim displayed a keen critical awareness that went beneath the surface meaning of the text. In her first response paper, Kim made what would be a typical move, monitoring her own reactions and constructing meaningful interpretation:

Reaction: "The Watcher Watched"
When I began reading this essay I thought it was a journal entry from a scientist. I expected a report about the behaviors and patterns of the den, based upon the writer's observations. I was completely uninterested in the essay. About halfway though I began to think the wolves were not the central focus. By the end of the essay, I felt the writer's realization of his own frailty compared to nature was the main message . . . perhaps the story is not about the wolves but about society. Perhaps man needs to look beyond myth and rumor to be open to finding the truth.

Kim's reactions to the readings are characterized by a fine self-awareness and an ability to make sharp distinctions: "I never expected the sentiments of gratitude," she writes about the reading "On Being Crippled"; "I empathize with the struggles the writer endures as a person rather than sympathize with her disability." She is also adept at construing irony: "I found it interesting that Ben Franklin, a man who's existence had a profound effect on our countries [*sic*] development, was so concerned with modesty." These skills bode well for the work that lay ahead after this crucial first semester.

Interestingly, in a more formal piece of writing for her U.S. history course, an essay on the Battle of Bataan that incorporates research, Kim's task is less interpretive than informational. Nevertheless, she refers to this as her favorite paper "just because it was fun . . . to just go out and start looking up all of this information, compiling it." "Bataan is a province, in the Philippines," begins a draft of this paper (the only version we saw), and it proceeds to describe the setting of the battle, the mission of the men assigned on the peninsula and the march that ensued. Quotations from various officers about the conditions during the battle and after the surrender of the Americans inform us of the humanitarian costs of the event. At no point are we given a case to be argued or presented with multiple perspectives on the battle. The mode is mostly narrative, albeit for the purpose of showing the hardships incurred by American soldiers: "Diseases like malaria and dysentery were rampid [*sic*]." It is only near the end of the paper that Kim begins to carve out a potential thesis or hypothesis: "The combined forces may have had a different survival rate had General McArthur [*sic*] chosen to stock pile supplies on the island." Little effort is made to substantiate the claim. That said, Kim did deploy her sources in effective ways:

> The conditions on the march were horrendous. The Japanese Army marched the men for days without food or water. As the days wore on men began to collapse from exhaustion Lieutenant Gene Boyt recalls, "As the men collapsed, one by one, they were killed and kicked into the borrow pits, along with the mud and feces" (Boyt 129). Men that fell behind on the march were killed. The Japanese army savagely beat the men and subjected them to extreme torture. The march lasted for five days, "Before the Death March was over. . . . Somewhere between 5,000 and 11,000 never made it to Camp O'Donnell, where fresh horrors awaited." (PBS)

Seeming comfortable employing signal phrases, well-chosen quotations, and in-text citations, Kim again displayed key academic skills, in this case the incorporation of relevant source material within her own writing.

But it is one thing to seek out and incorporate source materials for purposes of exposition. The research writing for her psychology course, Kim discovered, carried a different challenge. She notes a key feature of the writing done in psychology: "you're gonna find a theorist, and then find events in your life that support that particular theorist." The assignment, a research paper titled "Autobiography . . . and the Application of Erikson's Eight Stages of Development and Maslow's Hierarchy of Needs," required students to identify stressful events in their lives and discern some kind of developmental process in their narrative through application of theories of human development studied in the course. Oddly, the assignment allowed students to manufacture an event if "your own is too personal." This assignment mirrors what so often appears in a first-semester composition course when students are invited to write about their own lives in an effort to achieve student engagement and interest in their writing. But here, unlike in many composition courses, the narrative is put into the service of foregrounding a specific skill rather than serving the purpose of self-reflection. Here the goal is to demonstrate understanding of the theories of Erickson and Maslow through their application. We note the degree of complexity that the task represents: to hold both theories in the air, as it were, and then to test them in the laboratory of one's own psychological narrative. Of course, narrating a tale of hurt and estrangement is a significant challenge in and of itself. At least three pages of the paper were to be devoted to "personal development description" and at least two pages to "theorists and their theory."

In fact, Kim's ten-page "autobiography" privileged narrative over analysis, as over six pages told the story of the physical and psychological abuse that Kim experienced from both mother and father. She begins, "Black eyes, bruises and broken bones were a chronic condition for me as a child. Feelings of inferiority, desperation and worthlessness have haunted me for as far back as I can remember."

Kim tried to give the narrative a theoretical overlay by drawing subheadings from the textbook to universalize her account (for example, the first heading, a quotation from the textbook, reads, "'Psychological crisis leading to a lack of self-worth, guilt and mistrust [Myers 1998]'"). But, in fact, the narrative overwhelms any attempt at theory; both Kim and the reader are swept away by the violence described: "The last time my father beat me I was 15. He walked into my room called me a whore, pulled me out of bed by my hair, and spat in my face." It is only on page eight that Kim begins the process of applying Erickson's stage theory to her experience and even then the application amounts to a kind of question and answer format, rather than seamless analysis:

> **Trust vs. Mistrust; Autonomy vs. Shame and Doubt, Initiative vs. Guilt** (McGraw, 2005)—I do not remember anything prior to age 4. My grandmother recounts stories of me crying unattended for hours. I believe my inability to trust anyone or anything in my environment began at that time. I still struggle with entrusting my emotions and feelings with my loves [sic] ones. . . .

Kim uses the same approach with Maslow's Hierarchy of Needs, briefly asserting the application of theory to her life:

> **Safety Needs:** My earliest childhood memory indicates my lack of trust. I lived in a heightened state of awareness, leading to a state of constant distress. . . . Upon entering my grandmothers home my safety needs was [sic] met. I felt secure and stable. I began to interact with my peers.

It could be that Kim was struggling to predict her instructor's expectations. The instructions did not specify a seamless essay but rather apportions page lengths:

- At least 2 pages for theorists (2 theorists) and their theory—(10 points each theorist—if missing)
- 3 or more pages for personal development description

Kim likely assumed that the "personal development description" and the "pages for theorists" needed to be segregated rather than integrated. This experience serves as an exemplum of Kim's predicament in her first semester of college: she was ready to do the heavy lifting but was not given clear directions on how to do so. Recalling her statement during an interview, we are witnessing a student who dearly wants to know what a "perfect paper" looks like—enabling her then to produce the college-level work for which she was so clearly ready.

Kim experienced a third opportunity to conduct research, this time in her biology course for nonscience majors. Kim conducted research that was, again, informational. Her subject was red tide. The assignment was unconventional since Kim produced not a standard research paper but rather a desktop-published newsletter and brochure.

The newsletter is aimed at a technically savvy reader, somewhat conversant on the subject. Kim highlighted the four stages of "Harmful Algae Blooms (HABS)":

- First—Initiation. The dinoflagellate is introduced to the area
- Second—Reproduction. The algae blooms
- Third—Maintenance
- Fourth—Dissipation. The bloom disperses. Environmental factors like wind and current are a factor

Elsewhere Kim described the cellular structure of the algae as well as providing a chart depicting the variety of bloom likely in different parts of the country. The purpose is informational. A list of sources is given at the end but since no in-text citation is given in the body of the newsletter, it is hard to see what the sources did in the writing.

That is also the case with the brochure, although the references here are given merely as "Information Sites." What is most striking about the brochure is it represents a shift in audience and purpose. The intent here is less science and more public safety. One section, labeled "What is Red Tide?" provides essential information in everyday language:

The term "red tide" is used to refer to algae blooms that color the tide red. They occur when the nutrients in the water are bountiful and rapid cell division occurs. It is a natural occurring phenomenon.

On another panel, Kim described the effects of red tide, including the environmental, economic, and health-related consequences.

Fortunately for Kim and her classmates, the professor's expectations were laid out clearly in a grading rubric. Kim received full points (and a 95 percent overall) for the following categories:

- Major points are stated clearly, are supported by specific details, examples, or analysis; and are organized logically.
- The organization provides sufficient background on the topic and previews major points.
- Student has visual aids that complement presentation.
- Student shows confidence and mastery of topic researched during entire presentation.
- Sources are properly listed, including any website or personal interviews.

In the light of her stated desire to ground her writing in teachers' expectations, Kim must have found this rubric satisfying. She finally had a map to guide her in her ongoing academic journey. While clearly growing in confidence as a writer—desirous of obtaining and deploying control of her written work—Kim, by her own account, needed to know the parameters of what is allowable and what is possible. In that sense, she represents so many of our students: eager to succeed but needing the path laid out clearly.

BEN: CONFORMITY AND FREEDOM

Eighteen in the fall of 2007, Ben might seem to be a conventional first-semester college student. He came to the college directly after high school. He took four courses, a full-time load, that fall (achieving a 3.39 grade point average): accounting, College Writing, marketing, and math. He intended to major in business upon transferring to the local university. However, after interviewing Ben three times—twice in our office and once at lunch in the college cafeteria—we discovered him to be far more complex than the label "conventional student" might imply. Ben took night courses because he was working two jobs, one nearly full time (thirty-five hours) at a local Dunkin Donuts and the other at a radio station (ten to fifteen hours), where he assists his father. Living at home, Ben contributed to the family income. His sister was the first to have graduated from college in the family, although his mother had attended community college courses without graduating. Ben's father, a high school graduate, had taken certificate courses at the local vocational high school but had never taken college courses. Ben exhibited a maturity beyond his years. Having worked nearly full time since high school, Ben was paying his own way through college while assisting his family financially. He distinguished himself from other students his age who are "getting help from mom or dad" and for whom college is "just a part-time job."

When looking back—to just the previous semester—at his high school experience, Ben remarked on the "conformity" and strictness that defined those years for him. He savored the "freedom to roam" that college promises. With memories of high school so fresh, Ben freely volunteered what it was like to write in high school: "I found a lot of the writing, we couldn't use the personal pronoun 'I,' which I found difficult because they really, my teachers, didn't give us a solid lesson how to avoid using the pronoun. They just kind of threw it at us. Don't use 'I.' Good luck type of thing. . . . Kind of like being given a shovel and being told to dig holes but not where to dig them."

Obtaining pointed feedback was also a problem, Ben adds: "My high school English teacher, she had a tendency to just kind of say, 'You did this wrong.' Not how did I do it wrong; how do I need to fix it? As far as my English teacher this year, she had told me I'm wrong, but she has also explained to me how to fix it or what to do make [sic] it correct." As he begins his college career, Ben looks forward to receiving explicit instruction in how to improve his writing. He wants to have a clear and helpful explanation—when his writing works and when it doesn't: "I don't want to just see an 'X' . . . what's not right?"

By his own measure, Ben was asked to do a significant amount of writing in his first semester at college. While most of the writing was done in his English course ("every other week" in that class), Ben discloses two assignments not done in English: a collaboratively composed marketing plan and resume, assigned in his marketing and accounting classes, respectively. Speaking at length during an interview, Ben talked about the special requirements of writing a marketing plan: "We had to come up with a company and write a marketing plan for it, or we could take an already standing company . . . sections consisted of . . . mission goals, core competency . . . SWOT analysis [assessment of a company's strengths, weaknesses, opportunities, and threats], and . . . situational analysis."

While he did not include a copy of his marketing plan in his portfolio, Ben said he had "fun" with this project, mostly because (a) he found a partner that he could work productively with and (b) he and his partner had the license to construct a company from scratch. They enjoyed the opportunity to "take the helm of a company and make decisions."

For his accounting class, Ben was asked to draft a resume—a genre of writing assigned often in the college's career programs and technical courses. Ben decided to include copy in his portfolio. It is not clear whether what we read is a draft or not. What we do see is a pro forma and somewhat generalized work. While addressed to a specific advertising company and written in response to a "sales opening," the resume offers only cursory information about Ben's objectives and prior experience:

My Objective
My objective is to work for a company with growth in mind.
I want to work with goal driven and oriented individuals.

Professional Experience:
Financial Transaction Management—Successfully and repeatedly handled monetary transactions for a moderately sized franchise.

We can safely surmise that an eighteen-year-old student fresh from high school would see this exercise as premature, and Ben's writing suggests as much.

As a contrast, the writing for his composition course draws upon what Ben brings to the page: an account of an influential person in his life, for example, or strongly held and personalized views on advertising or the harassment of one student by another. The writing prompts followed a conventional, modal approach: Ben and his classmates were asked to write essays demonstrating exemplification, narration, definition, and classification. In addition, Ben produced a rhetorical analysis of a reading—looking at a reading's main ideas, purpose and audience, and style and structure.

The first assignment of the course required Ben to write a "descriptive/narrative essay . . . a 500 word essay about a person, place or event that significantly changed your life." Ben obliged with this initial draft:

> Many people say their father is an important person in their life and has changed their life in a positive way so they can get a good grade. Due to my father's career choice, he has inspired me to continue in his footsteps. To be honest, he really has affected my life in a positive way. If you will bear with me for a little while, I can show you many more ways he has affected my life in a positive way.
>
> To begin, my father has always pushed me to succeed in school. When I would procrastinate on assignments, he would be there to give me a figurative slap in the head and get me on track. Also, if I was failing a class, he would be on the phone and in touch with my teachers to find out why. When it came to college, he was instrumental in picking my college major, and I was happy about that. When I have a big money job, I will owe that success to my father.
>
> My father was instrumental in me getting my first job. Even when I thought I would never get hired anywhere, my father told me to keep on these people about my application. You know what, I have been working at a Dunkin's Donuts for two years now. I appreciate what my father has helped me to achieve in my life so far.

In addition, I vaguely mentioned my father's career inspiring me to follow in his footsteps. My father's career choice was Broadcasting or working in radio, in laymen's words. I used to get to go on the job with him a lot when I was a kid and he showed me how much fun and how little like a job radio can be. Radio is so much more like a hobby than a job and I loved it! He has met celebrities and presidents through his chosen career. When I finish school and get into the work world I want to be able to look back and parallel my father's my [*sic*] career and see a mirror image, if not a better image on my side of the mirror.

Lastly, my father was always there to help when I was in need. When I had issues with other kids at school, my father always stepped up to the plate and defended my honor with all he had. If ever I needed anything at all he was there. For that I am more grateful than my pen can make words to describe how I feel.

To conclude, in my eyes my father is the man. Assistant, guide, defender, superhero, and magic man are all words that I use to describe who my father is to me. If I don't read it to him though, I don't think he would, nor anyone else could understand what he means to me. To finalize this piece of hopefully good writing, my father is a man who has positively influenced my life. I love Him.

We quote the full draft to show Ben capable of analysis and exhibiting a sense of structure from the outset of the course. After announcing his father as the subject of the essay, the paper offers separate paragraphs, each focusing on a discrete area shaped by his father's influence: school, job, career, and social needs. A superficial series of transitional terms ("To begin . . . In addition . . . Lastly") alerts us to a sequencing of subtopics. Ben's instructor responded favorably to this draft: "good narrative essay, well organized." The paper received a B+ with the reward of an A- upon revision. On the second draft, the instructor makes the relatively minor changes herself, chiefly from the first and last paragraphs:

Many people say their father is an important person in their life and has changed their life in a positive way. ~~I can honestly say that my father has affected my life in many positive ways from success in school, to getting my first job, and my career choice~~ so they can get a good grade. Due to my father's career choice, he has inspired me to continue in his foot steps. ~~To be honest, he really has affected my life in a positive way. If you will bear with me for a little while, I can show you many more ways he has affected my life in a positive way.~~

. . . ~~To conclude,~~ ~~I~~in my eyes my father is the man. Assistant, guide, defender, superhero, and magic man are all words that I use to describe who my father is to me. As I sit here and write this, I know what I am saying would bring him to tears. If I don't read it to him though, I don't think he would, nor anyone else could understand what he means to me. ~~To finalize this piece of hopefully good writing,~~ ~~M~~my father is a man who has positively influenced my life, and~~;~~ I love Him for it.

We're not certain that this kind of teacherly intervention with his text was what Ben had in mind when asking for explicit help from his instructors (something he felt he had not received in high school). Rather than allow Ben to begin informally and thus write his way into this subject, the instructor insists on a standard introduction that announces the topical classification to come. The instructor becomes the editor of Ben's writing, crossing out infelicities of style and inserting preferred phrasing. Dutifully, Ben reproduced the changes in a third draft and received the promised A-. Our focus here is on Ben's writing, but the instructor's decision to co-opt that writing raises interesting pedagogical questions about appropriate teacher commentary on student writing—a subject we discuss in our chapter on faculty practices.

We may infer from her comments on this paper that the instructor would prefer Ben to frontload his argument in his introductory paragraph. Ben complies in the writing that follows, as we see here in the introduction to his classification paper on drivers:

Drivers, you can't live with them, and you can't live without them. With them you have a hell of a hard time keeping patience while driving. Without them, car salesmen would no one [*sic*] to sell cars to. There are a few categories I can classify them under, they are: Death drivers, senior drivers, No License drivers, Cut and Slow drivers, and lastly, good drivers. These category names may make no sense, but they will when I explain them.

Given the perfunctory classification at the start and the clichéd (to us, at any rate, if not to an eighteen-year old) opening statement, we might well surmise that Ben has become a formulaic writer, eager to please his instructor and to reside within the box of academic convention. But it becomes clear, as we read on, that Ben exhibits not only a fine self-consciousness about language ("Senior drivers really need to get up to speed with driving [pun intended]") but a desire to take risks ("when you have that moron behind you who must be touching your bumper"). We might construe the latter quality as a mere failure to achieve the appropriate register, but evidence elsewhere in his portfolio suggests otherwise.

We note the level of comfort and risk taking that Ben displays in his definition essay, "I am Better Than You," the first two paragraphs of which we quote below:

> I entered college this year as a first year student and I thought everything would be different. I thought everyone would be mature and everyone would treat each other with respect. I thought very, very WRONG. I sit here in the writing lab just one hour and forty minutes away from the start of class. I learn very quickly that what I thought had ended, is still very much alive. Harassment, I saw it in elementary school, I saw it in middle school, I saw it in high school, and I still see it in college. It is utterly depressing. Harassment is defined in the Benjamin Dictionary as: any form of bringing someone's self esteem down in order to boost one's own self-esteem.
>
> As I said, I am sitting here in the writing lab in K building hurriedly typing my Definition essay to have it done for 4PM.

As I begin this essay I plan to talk about racism; then plans change. I hear two young gentlemen who are students here talking: One says to the other, "Do I have a story for you. I was walking through the campus when I overheard two girls talking. One said to the other about how tiring it was to walk from class to class. So I chimed in, I bet it is carrying all that fatty fat round with you!" How messed up is that. Then I take a look to see the kid who said it and he is not in any position to be talking about anyone's weight issue himself. I found what he said very offensive, though I did not say anything because it wasn't my conversation to be involved and I wasn't there for the incident or I would have said something if I was there for the initial offense.

Ben goes on to argue that such off-hand comments stand in for cultural expectations affecting women's self-imagery, imagery that often has little basis in objective reality ("I feel bad for these girls that weigh like 120 pounds"). On its face, such a claim shows the writer's significant maturity. But that maturity is on display on a stylistic level as well. We note, for starters, the forcefulness of the essay's title—and its ironic content: those who define others unfairly are hardly "better." We see the carefully wrought parallel and purposefully repetitive structure of his phrasing, "I saw it in elementary school, I saw it in middle school, I saw it in high school, and I still see it in college." We remark as well the ironically self-deprecating phrase "the Benjamin Dictionary": signaling an intention to take the task, but not himself, too seriously (after all, others may have their own "dictionary" and words are so often subjectively used and received). We recognize also that Ben admits in writing to drafting his paper the afternoon it is due and switching his topic at the last minute. He is surely not the first student to do such. But why write about these acts? We conjecture that Ben demonstrates some admirable writerly qualities: flexibility and self-reflexivity. In other words, he is, by his own admission, open to changes of direction when writing and able to monitor, in a self-conscious way, those changes. Ben writes about his writing: unlike less experienced writers, who remain in the "writer-based" perspective, Ben is both writer and reader here, cognizant of writing in the act of composing (Flower; Armstrong). Underlying both qualities is of course confidence in his own abilities, confidence that produced an A for the course. We would add that Ben exhibits a situational or rhetorical perspective when he writes, "I did not say anything because it wasn't my conversation to be involved and *I wasn't there for the incident* or I would have said something if I was there for the initial offense" (emphasis ours). Robert Kegan, whom we referenced earlier, might refer to Ben's thinking as achieving the "Third Order of Consciousness" (28). In other words, Ben thinks relationally rather than in isolation. He could have dismissed these students' behaviors categorically but instead made his charges of harassment and hurtful stereotyping contingent upon "being there." He thus offers these students the benefit of doubt. Ben judges these students, to be sure, but he knows the difference between being present and being absent when confronting others' actions and states of mind. Describing the various capabilities of those who achieve the "Third Principle" of understanding, Kegan writes that such knowers can "reason abstractly, that is, reason about reasoning; think hypothetically . . . be aware of shared feelings, agreements, and expectations that take primacy over individual interests . . . internalize another's point of view" (30–31).

In writing to meet his teachers' demands, Ben does not comprise his own individual interests. Rather he sees them in relationship with others'. He can conform to academic convention without yielding his "freedom to roam."

NICOLE: BETWEEN PLACES

A traditional-aged student, Nicole registered for fifteen credits of coursework in the fall of 2007, including College Writing, introduction to management, economics, history, and math. She withdrew from economics and history some weeks into the semester, becoming, officially, a part-time student.

While she was beginning her college education, her parents were both making career shifts. Her mother earned a college degree and acquired a position as a nurse, which Nicole thought was a "huge change" for the family. One change, she explained, was that her mother was "happier and healthier." Her father was trying to start his own business at this time, telling Nicole, "If you want to make a lot of money, you have to be your own boss." Both of her parents were supportive of Nicole's decision to attend college.

Her goal to earn a business degree seemed a logical extension of her familial experience and high school education. A graduate of a technical high school, Nicole studied to become a hair dresser, the profession in which she was currently employed. When asked why she decided to attend Bristol, she explained that admissions counselors visited her high school to do "on the spot" admissions, where students were allowed to fill out applications for free. She felt this was the main impetus behind her decision.

Although Nicole was a friendly and outgoing person, she felt as though she was going through college alone, which was difficult for her. Despite her involvement in this study, she felt disconnected from faculty, staff, and other students at BCC. Worse still, she was intimidated by professors, especially, she said, those who don't provide contact information (or encourage contact) such as e-mail addresses. These faculty, she felt, don't want to help her. This was an issue for some of the classes in which she was assigned writing, as she hesitated to ask her professors for clarification about work in progress. She chose instead to seek advice from peer and professional tutors.

Nicole did a small amount of writing in courses outside of College Writing. The writing assignments in management and economics— two in each course—didn't seem to have stringent requirements. Regarding a biography assigned by her management professor, she explained, "He didn't really give us a specific amount of pages. I think it had to be at least three pages or something like that . . . it didn't have to be in any sort of form." In economics, Nicole "didn't get to revise [papers]. . . . I don't think he really cared what order . . . I mean it had to be in a paragraph form, but other than that I didn't get any comments on anything, really. He just told me, 'It was good.'" This writing seemed to be informational in nature, with topics including the European Union and the extinction of honey bees. The goal of these assignments seemed to be acquiring—and learning—course content. Each required the use of sources, though not the evaluation of those sources.

One assignment in economics allowed Nicole to respond/react. In this assignment, she argued, as a Wampanoag, for a casino in southeastern Massachusetts: "I can't help but feel for them and there [*sic*] land being taken away. Personally, I think they should receive more than a casino." This paper, written in the first week of the semester, was submitted once and received no feedback save for a "check plus" at the top of the first page. Nicole eventually dropped this course.

Despite her interest in business, it was writing in her College Writing course—not in management or economics—that she enjoyed the most. There she composed no fewer than ten essays, with multiple drafts of each. At least nine of these received written feedback from her professor. One particularly memorable piece for Nicole was the essay in which she described "the halls of [her] own high school." She "described how the different students acted," which was easy, she explained, because she "hated [her] high school . . . [and she] could describe things [she] hated really good."

Nicole thought that communication about her writing progress was limited, at times, in terms of written feedback on papers, and she was looking for direction in this regard. The exception, perhaps not surprisingly, was her College Writing course. To get her point across about limited feedback, she referenced the biography she did for management. The only comment related to her referring to the subject too informally: "I called Frederick Taylor, 'Fred,' and [the professor] got mad at me because he's like professional and you're not supposed to call him by a nickname." When asked whether she perceived such limited feedback to be a good thing, Nicole replied, "No. Even if you didn't like it, I'd rather him write more because he didn't give me, like, I mean, I didn't get a bad grade, but I still would like to know . . . I don't think he just marked me down for just calling him 'Fred,' you know? I'd rather know so I can fix my writing better, especially. I don't think I'm very good at biographies, so that is one thing I do want to improve on."

Not having done much writing in high school, she was looking for development and guidance in this regard. While in high school, her teachers responded mainly to surface errors, "grammar and spelling." She recalled, "We never got to revise."

Writing in high school involved applying a rigid formula. As Nicole remembers, "The beginning paragraph had to be a certain number of sentences and then the body had to be four paragraphs and then the conclusion had to restate everything." She questioned writing in this manner, saying, "I don't think it's right. I don't know. Just . . . writing should be like how you feel, I think." Writing should "get your point across" and "keep the reader interested."

Early in the fall semester, her College Writing course was already influencing her writing process. Nicole thinks the most significant impact involved invention strategies. She explains, "Freewriting. I never really did that before, but it helps me a lot because when you freewrite it gets all your ideas down. And then you can just go and pick out all the things that really make sense." She was composing two or three drafts of a paper at this point, though changes were limited to fixing "punctuation mistakes. I tend to make a lot of those. I insert commas wherever I feel like it."

By semester's end, Nicole thought she'd learned quite a bit about writing, partly because of the variety of tasks performed: "I learned from a lot of things. Honestly, I haven't done most of the writing that we did in here [in her college writing course]. I never had to do . . . description. . . . You know what I mean. Different topics." She emphasized freewriting again: "I realized that it really is [necessary] because if you don't write down all your ideas and you forget them all when you try to put everything together because I said I'm a perfectionist, so I try to make everything perfect and then I forget it."

She also thought she was better able to develop her ideas and know when to do so, what her professor referred to as amplification. Nicole explained, "Before . . . I didn't know where to bring those extra details to make the paper better." When asked how she now goes about identifying the need for more "details," she discussed seeking reader feedback: "usually I let it go to another person and have them read my writing. If they don't really understand it, then most of the time it's not really that I did something wrong. It's that I didn't provide enough details, and I didn't know that before." Note here as well that her writing isn't "correct" or "incorrect," "right" or "wrong," but malleable.

Right from the first paper she wrote in her College Writing course, Nicole's professor called for her to amplify her ideas. Although the first draft submitted earned a grade of B, she was encouraged to revise further in the end comment: "What you have here is good. To make it even better, consider amplifying—supplying additional examples and details. I've indicated the problem spots, so check my comments and corrections throughout—feel free to revise." The "comments and corrections" were abundant, and included positive reactions (for example, "Good conclusion"), instructions/corrections (for example, "When you shift focus, begin a new paragraph"), and suggestions (for example, "I'm not sure what you mean here. Re-state and explain."). There weren't any explicit calls for additional detail within the in-text comments, although there were two places where clarification was needed. Her next draft earned an A-, but the professor's comments indicated where further amplification was needed, the in-text comments clearly indicating a connection between the reader's lack of understanding and the need for the author to "amplify." Nicole seemed to be gaining a valuable lesson early on about the need to develop ideas to clearly communicate meaning to the target audience—here, the professor.

About a month later, Nicole wrote what she considered her best piece in this course, one in which she described the "halls" of her old high school, reproduced exactly as submitted:

I Stand and Look Out

I am an observer of human behavior and actions. This year I graduated from Old Colony Reg. Voc. Tech. High School where I observed many students who walk down the hall ways. Human behavior really interests me, but it also depresses me. It depresses me because I often envision myself in other peoples [*sic*] shoes and feel others' pain as though it's mine. The reason I observe human behavior is because I feel that it is my duty as a Christian woman to watch over my brothers and sisters, and learn from their mistakes.

In my memory I stand and look out upon the sadness of Old Colony, and upon all the oppression and shame. I hear, in the halls of my school, the secret weeping of the friendless. In the cafeteria, six tables have teenagers always looking behind their back. Three tables have one student at each end of each table, maybe a few in the middle but still distant from the others, not speaking but a few words to each other. Many sit alone. They are alone in the cafeteria, but they also feel alone inside. They are depressed because they are bullied or friendless. They dress differently or maybe they listen to different music or have different hobbies. Some have disabilities and some are just a little shy. In any case, they are different and that's why they sit alone.

I see them now. The hollow-eyed and lonely students paint on smiles to conceal their tears. They try to "fit in." They have to pretend they have a lot of friends in order to actually make friends. I stand and watch the loving and kind hearted being martyred by the cruelty of hatred. I see and feel the grief.

Can you hear the whispers? Although the whispers are soft, they are very sharp. These whispers can pierce the soul. These whispers are lies that the teens are spreading so they won't be the scapegoat of the class. Quick! It's a race to see who can totally destroy a persons' self-esteem before *they* get looked at as less than perfect.

I see the prejudice, cliques, jealousy, and self-centeredness of teens roaming the halls. I also see the bullying of the people too weak to follow their own dreams. Everywhere I look there is stealing and cheating. In every corner and every room, girls are being looked upon like nothing by the boys. The girls are letting themselves be misused. I feel pity and heartache.

I observe the world around me, but my strongest memories of observing human behavior is in Old Colony. I can easily see, hear, and feel all the hatred, jealousy, selfishness, helplessness and pain without end inside those high school walls. I could make high school more enjoyable to some students by befriending the friendless and speaking the truth, but as for all the rest, I can only learn from their mistakes.

Her professor responded positively to this draft, and she earned an A-. Both marginal and summative comments prompted further revision despite the initial success. She was asked to amplify the ideas in her third paragraph. Nicole did revise, but the third paragraph remained unchanged as she mainly attended to surface corrections.

This stylistically advanced piece provides evidence that Nicole is somewhere between Kegan's second and third stages of development. While she is aware of her own belief system "as a Christian woman," she doesn't lay out precisely what those beliefs are, nor does she indicate how she was implicated in the proceedings. Judging the actions of others, Nicole doesn't turn a critical lens inward. She seems to consider the beliefs and actions of those who whisper as counter to her own, incorrect, and unchanging. She shows, nevertheless, in this piece that she is becoming more aware of how she views the world even though that self isn't fully manifest in the writing. Through its pathetic appeal, her essay would likely solicit the most support from an audience with shared beliefs.

Papers written early in the semester underwent, generally, a two-draft process. Changes were made between the first and second drafts submitted, but there were two drafts in most cases and changes tended to be limited to grammar and mechanics. (Only when the first draft earned an A was there just a single draft.)

This process evolved over time. The research paper, for example, received its first round of feedback in the latter half of October and was resubmitted at the end of the course. The extensive changes made to this piece may indicate a deepened understanding of the revision process and the needs of readers. Initially, her professor called for amplification at the end of her second paragraph, which read,

Many parents all over the world argue that their religious freedom is being violated when doctors act against their wishes (and religion) by providing medical treatment to their children that could save their lives. To this day, doctors who are convinced that a child is being denied needed medical treatment can lodge a complaint with the government. Doing this can get a court order that requires the treatment (Coggins, par 8). This has been done a number of times in Canada to require transfusions for children of Jehovah's Witnesses. "Jehovah's Witnesses believe that the Bible says that they should 'abstain from blood' (Acts 21:25), and therefore refuse blood transfusions for themselves and their children" (Coggins, par. 6).

In the next draft submitted, Nicole elaborates quite a bit, continuing the paragraph after the ending quote and adding a new paragraph:

> Many children of Jehovah's Witnesses are dying when they could have had a chance at life. It is unfortunate that these parents choose religion over their own children's lives.
>
> Another instance in which the state courts ordered hospital care was for a child whose father was a minister in the Church of God. This twelve-year-old had a rare form of bone cancer and was told by doctors that without chemotherapy and radiation treatment she would die within months. As a member of the Church of God of the union Assembly fundamentalist sect, this child is not permitted to seek medical treatment; the church councils their members to rely on prayer to heal them. After receiving medical treatment the child was said to have no more evidence of the cancer. The state is trying to save lives of the children being neglected and that means they are putting a limit on religious freedom (Ostling, par. 1).

These additions include Nicole's own conclusions/assertions as well as an additional example to indicate that the issue she was concerned with involved more than one religion. She added additional examples throughout the piece—amplifying—in response to the feedback she'd received. Changes were limited, however, to those suggested by her professor. Her efforts earned her an A.

Not only had she made advances in terms of development, she had also made strides in owning her writing. While Nicole responded somewhat passively to the feedback she'd received on her first paper, she had questions about the suggestions made on the next paper she submitted and received back. Though she doesn't wish for details of this piece to be discussed due to the personal nature of the narrative, her concerns were twofold. One, the professor was asking her to "correct" the spelling of a cultural term—a term she assured us was spelled correctly, and two, she didn't want to do what she felt she had been asked to do in the margin near her opening paragraph: "You might want to hint that a particular event makes your memories worse." She explained, "I don't want to do that." And she didn't. Her next draft remained unchanged in response to these comments.

Interestingly, Nicole didn't seem aware that she had begun to make such decisions. Unlike Kim, when asked how she uses feedback, Nicole didn't indicate a desire to maintain ownership, to decide which responses to act upon: "I definitely pay attention to the things that people write, because . . . I don't know how to really answer that question. I like the feedback. It helps and I like every time somebody says something about my writing; I always try to remember it. And then I look at it in every single paper that I do." She elaborated further, saying, "Once I realized something, I would fix them in the next paper, because that's what the teacher told us to do. I followed it pretty good, I think."

Such a response may indicate that Nicole has yet to bridge over into cross-categorical thinking. Instead of actively engaging with the feedback she received, carefully considering alternative ideas and approaches, she seemed content to deliver what was expected. Working toward such objectivity provides her and many other students in our classrooms with a challenge, one that, we think, can only be met with guiding feedback that encourages student ownership.

WENDY: WRITING WITHIN THE LINES

In the fall of 2007, Wendy was a forty-year-old student at Bristol taking her first college course, English 10: Basic Writing. She was working full time while helping to care for her family, a husband and two sons, making understandable her decision to register for a course that met on Friday nights from 7:00 to 9:40 P.M.

Family supported her return to school. She explained, "The boys, my husband [told me] . . . 'You can do whatever you want to do.'" A related source of motivation was her boys' bearing witness to their mother's efforts to further educate herself. While her husband provided verbal encouragement despite not having attended college or receiving a high school diploma, Wendy, through her actions, provides her children a daily reminder of the importance of education. She explains, "When I came back to school, it helped my boys to see, 'Hey, mom's doing it too!' You know? And she's sitting down and doing her homework and I'm learning at the same time."

Wendy's day as a working mother and part-time student is a busy one: "It was work all day, do your homework, makes sure their homework was done, clean your house, you know, check on Loretta [a sick neighbor]. It was a lot. It was a lot, you know? And working with a new job . . . I didn't have a deputy at the time, and when I get a deputy, I'm training the deputy, so it was a lot." Despite a hectic schedule, or perhaps because of it, Wendy welcomed her weekly class meeting for basic writing: "I'd stop at Dunkin Donuts to get a cup of coffee and go upstairs . . . in K building, sit up in that little area and just pull out my little notebook and write."

While a student in Basic Writing Skills, she was asked to compose six formal papers, keep a journal in which she would write in and out of class (the aforementioned "little notebook"), and demonstrate her end-of-semester writing abilities in a "final writing." Though the instructor explained in the course syllabus that students would first "concentrate on the basics, sentences and paragraphs," and eventually move to essays, the first and subsequent assignments required "5 paragraph essays." This doesn't seem to have concerned Wendy, despite considering her writing ability "dreadful." She composed a number of essays during the semester, and each draft submitted to the instructor was assigned a grade on a ten-point scale. Revision was encouraged, and Wendy was pleased to know that she could rework her writing to improve the grade.

When asked to write a paper about "an everyday annoyance in your life," Wendy had a great time composing the first draft of a paper detailing some of her husband's junkyard projects. This paper, wonderfully titled "One Man's Junk is Another Man's Junk," sarcastically and confidently describes three current projects. The first involves splicing together two vehicles:

> His first project has been going on for approximately three years and I see no end in site. He has two vans to make into one. So, in the front of my garage is a whole van and a chasse of another. Scattered throughout the garage are an assortment of parts including springs, tires, bushings and a motor taken from one of the vans. The other van is still in tact, just waiting its turn to be dissected or a better word would be cannibalized. He said, "I will use this van as an everyday vehicle." I hope his "working" truck does not break down before the van is completed.

Pleased with her first draft, she was disheartened to learn that her instructor thought that she had strayed from her focus. In fact, he didn't think her paper included the required thesis as the last sentence of her opening paragraph. Here she had written, "Looking around my yard and garage reminds me of Sanford and Son's junkyard."

The assignment had called for body paragraphs that would, according to the prompt, "be the support details." The body of her essay does seem to include ample detail: "The strewn parts include but are not limited to an assortment of hoods, motors, fenders and grills. He has taken pieces from all the tractors reshaped and molded them back into the original shape. Some parts have been primed, painted and covered with blankets to keep them safe." Her recurring sarcasm, evident in phrases such as "The excitement of all of this is mind-boggling, to say the least" and the title of the essay seem an attempt to get at the writing prompt's required focus on an everyday annoyance, but her instructor wonders about whether she'd focused appropriately: "The details here are very well shown, but why are they being shown? What is the focus (thesis) of the essay? The details do well in showing how much 'junk' there is, but the annoyance of it all isn't clear yet."

In her next draft, Wendy seems to be addressing her instructor's feedback. Her opening paragraph has a new final line, perhaps an attempt to include an acceptable thesis: "It makes my blood boil, stomach spin and angry." In conversation, Wendy explained that this isn't really the case; she considers her husband's obsession with fixing up junk cars to be a lovable quirk as opposed to an infuriating habit. This emerging writer was struggling with how to respond to the feedback she received while still retaining a level of ownership (albeit creative nonfiction) of the writing. She admitted frustration at hearing again, on this second draft, that she needed a tighter focus. Paragraph four, which explained the third of her husband's current projects, was questioned: "How does this [paragraph] support point 3? Anger?" Here the instructor seemed to be referring to Wendy's newly constructed thesis that listed three interwoven feelings, different degrees of displeasure: boiling blood, a spinning stomach, and anger. The fourth paragraph apparently needed to focus on anger; it currently didn't seem to do so:

> Lastly, he buys more vehicles than we need. His latest prize, mind you the fee he paid for this treasure (sight unseen) was a fortune of five ($5.00) dollars! He is going to restore a 1993 Ford E350 Cube Van, gasoline engine, 3 speed automatic, 85,000 miles, in running condition with (oh yes) rotten rear body rails. Just the thought of this gem makes me sick to my stomach. More "junk" to add to the collection for me to look at.

The instructor identified the penultimate sentence as relating to "point #2," her "spinning stomach," though arguably Wendy has but one point she is trying to make.

In our discussions about this piece, Wendy revealed that responding to her instructor's feedback took the "fun" out of the writing. While she may eventually be able to enjoy writing while still delivering what the instructor is looking for, Wendy admits to having difficulty doing both. Her efforts to fit the expected formula were successful, however; earlier drafts earned an eight out of ten points, but her last revision of this piece earned ten out of ten points. This final draft follows, reproduced as submitted, with track changes indicating material added since the previous draft:

One Man's Junk Is Another Man's Junk

Looking at van parts, tractor parts and truck parts is very annoying to me. I call all of these parts "junk." My husband is an avid collector of all of these various parts. He has always worked on vehicles since he was young and enjoys the task. Looking around my yard and garage reminds me of "Sanford and Son's" junkyard. It makes my blood boil, stomach spin and feel very angry.

My blood begins to boil when I look at my husband's first project. The van project has been going on for approximately three years. He has two vans to make into one. So, in the front of my garage is a whole van and a chasse of another. Scattered throughout the garage are an assortment of parts including springs, tires, bushings and a motor taken from one of the vans. It is a total eye sore.

The second project makes my stomach tumble. He has begun making a tractor for pulling events. He has approximately four (4) tractors to combine into one. The strewn parts from this project include, but are not limited to, an assortment of hoods, motors, fenders and grills. He has taken pieces from all the tractors, and reshaped and molded them back into the original shape. Some parts have been primed, painted and covered with blankets to keep them safe. Just the thought of his gems make me sick to my stomach. I would not be so aggravated about this mess if he would finish a project.

Lastly, he buys more vehicles than we need. His latest prize, sight unseen, was a fortune of five ($5.00) dollars. He is going to restore a 1993 Ford E350 Cube Van, gasoline engine, 3 speed automatic, 85,000 miles, in running condition with (oh yes) rotten rear body rails. My patience with all of his collection is very short. I know that I am sarcastic to him about his treasures. I always have a sarcastic remark to him concerning his treasures. I say comments such as "not more junk," "what will be done with that rusty piece of junk" and

"I see you brought more junk to add to the collection for me to look at." My remarks about his holey empire are brought on because of my anger.

I cannot stand looking around my yard at all of this "junk." I do admit he is a very good mechanic but never seems to finish a project whether it is a van, tractor or truck endeavor. I know that the garage and surrounding area are full of valuable parts in his mind and the mind of others. I have even intercepted numerous phone calls from speed-shops asking if we had a variety of parts in stock. To keep my sanity, I have decided, that if I ever win the lottery, I will purchase my husband his own junkyard, of course, miles from my home.

Wendy's instructor responded to this revision concisely with only an end comment: "Excellent revision. This is much more cohesive." Through working on this first piece, Wendy was learning to mold her writing, making slight adjustments to conform to her instructor's expectations. The new sentences in paragraphs three and four, for example, seem to respond to earlier comments about focus. Though the new sentence in paragraph two seems to connect to the main idea of the paragraph, it isn't so clear that the new sentences in paragraph four are as successful. Still, Wendy seems to be trying to stick to the series of ideas presented in her thesis.

For subsequent writing assignments, Wendy e-mailed her instructor a couple paragraphs to make sure she was on the right track: "I was thinking [that] maybe I just wasn't understanding what I was supposed to do . . . I figured, 'Why write the whole paper?' . . . and then find out . . . it wasn't really what he wanted." This process was new to her, as she'd learned you needed to pass work in for feedback: "when I went to high school, the only thing I remember is you write your paper and then you go back and revise it, and the only input you're going to get is after you turn it in."

Although Wendy seemed to rely heavily on her instructor's feedback, the focus of that feedback, for the drafts we were privileged to read, turned more toward grammar and phrasing issues, particularly toward the last third of the semester. The last paper submitted, titled "Adventure," had a peer review sheet attached with a classmate's feedback. What is interesting is that the questions posed by the instructor on the peer review sheet don't seem to be the criteria used by the instructor upon his reading of her draft. He asks in the peer review questions, for example, "What point is the writer making about the essay's subject?" and "Does the writer include enough detail?" Though there is, later, one question that hints at stylistic choices involving language and sentence structure, comments on Wendy's draft were limited to identifying four sentence-level errors, two phrasing issues, five wrong-word errors, two verb tense errors, two corrections on the use of semicolons and colons, and one proper noun needing capitalization.

This feedback suggests that Wendy's paper needed only final polishing. Given the focus earlier in the semester on establishing a clear link between thesis and support, it was interesting here that there weren't comments relating to just such an issue. Her paper begins with what seems to be a thesis (though it is recommended by the instructor that this sentence end the introductory paragraph): "My first adventure out on my own left me cold, sacred [*sic*] and in a lot of trouble." She goes on to offer context and to tell the story of her running away from home at the age of five. There are relevant details, for sure, such as her mother's demands on her time that caused her to leave and the climate and landscape experienced upon her departure from the farmhouse. Numerous other details aren't so clearly relevant, such as her suitcase that was "11 x 14 inch the size of legal size copy paper, a pretty yellow and green plaid with a petite black handle" or the description of her favorite doll. These details fail to receive comment; in fact, the end comment begins, "Great use of details in this narrative." Also not commented upon is the focus on physical events as opposed to emotional responses, as suggested by the opening paragraph and thesis. Though she does relay a frightening sequence, being out in the cold with the sun setting, this section doesn't receive special emphasis. After these events, her experience at a neighbor's house snacking on milk and cookies seemed more enjoyable than frightening. When she does get back to a scene that relates to her thesis, specifically getting into a lot of trouble, she ends her paper. More work could have been done to produce a "cohesive" essay, though the feedback doesn't encourage such reenvisioning.

Her previous paper focused on detail and description, so it is understandable that there might be more details than may have been needed in this next assignment. In fact, Wendy considered the previous assignment a valuable learning experience: "The last one that I wrote was about my grandparents. We had to do a descriptive essay, so I was able to describe what their house was at that time, and now I know all the changes to it, and they're deceased. It brought back a lot of memories, so that I really liked." From this descriptive essay assignment, Wendy was learning to keep her audience's needs in mind, in this case to be able to share something personal with strangers: "It made me think that when I'm describing it, I need to make sure that the person that's reading it can see it. That really makes you think when you're writing it and when you're rereading it, you know?" Wendy saw how this lesson would benefit her at work, to more effectively consider what readers of her commendations and proclamations would need to know.

This experience in basic writing seems to have been both satisfying and educational, as Wendy attempted to register for the next course in the sequence, College Writing, the following semester. Unfortunately, there was no course scheduled for the Friday evening time slot she preferred, so she continues to wait for such an offering.

In response to what transpired in her English course, Wendy has changed the way she approaches writing tasks. For instance, she now creates an outline before starting to write as opposed to generating a "mess," as she believes she did previously. Wendy also does freewriting now and uses this with the outline to start her draft. Perhaps most interestingly, she has grown to depend on the feedback process, which influenced future papers: "You think, he wrote this on my paper when I did this, so maybe I should reread that. And, I mean, take out the word 'you' and don't use contractions. All of those things kind of pop in when I'm writing anything." This was a change from previous schooling, as her college instructor was clearer about what he meant in marginal and end comments: "I don't think high school teachers are as in-tune to the students as college professors . . . when I was there. . . . They would just write something in the margin. You get your grade and here you go. That's it, you know? So they don't explain to you why, and when you're in high school, you're not going to go up and ask. They don't explain what you need to work on."

Wendy, in her own words, "wanted to come back to school to freshen up on [her] writing skills," which would help her in her current position as town clerk. In this position, she "write[s] a lot of proclamations and commendations." She enjoys the commendations more than the proclamations and ordinances she works on: "it's fun because you're writing about another person and what they've done, and you have a list of what they've done, and you can incorporate all that. And the ordinances aren't as much fun. They are very strict. You know, you have to research, and they're not as much fun . . . some of the proclamations that we have that are coming up. . . . We do them every year, so we just kind of change a few things." Here too, as with some of the writing we discussed in her basic writing course, Wendy seemed aware that the need for "correct" structure or format limits the writer's choices, in her words, the "fun," the freedom to play with ideas and words. When the course was over, Wendy concluded, "When you're writing something, it needs to be fun." It is, perhaps, that writing with which Wendy finds herself most engaged. She also seems aware, however, that there are times when it is necessary to follow the prescribed formula—whether a five-paragraph essay or a proclamation.

ANDREW: ENCOUNTERING NEW GENRES

Andrew, an eighteen-year-old traditional student, is the second in his family to attend Bristol. His sister earned an associate's degree in occupational therapy in the mid-1990s. Though he wanted to follow in his brother's footsteps and have a career in the military, a back problem disqualified him from service. He has since decided to pursue a career in politics, currently working to attend law school and become an attorney. In addition to seeking a formal degree, Andrew serves on two municipal committees, demonstrating a strong concern with local political issues.

A focused individual, Andrew selected courses commensurate with his career pursuits. In the fall, he was enrolled in College Writing, U.S. history, U.S. government and politics, and algebra. His portfolio for the fall 2007 semester included writing from two of those courses, College Writing and U.S. history.

Andrew seemed fairly confident about his writing abilities at the start of the semester, a perception that may have limited his openness to suggestions about changes to his drafts and writing processes: "I think my writing ability is pretty strong. Overall, I've had some good experiences in the past with high school and middle school writing, so I think I can always develop my skills in writing I think with more experienced professors and teachers, giving me advice in how to write papers or write better papers. I can do so but I think for the most part my skills are pretty well developed."

Writing that requires some measure of reflection piqued Andrew's interest more than that requiring summary only. His memoir in College Writing allowed him to do such reflection and include his reaction to the events on September 11, 2001. He had limited opportunities to do this type of work in high school: "most of the writing that I had, that I conducted in high school was more on summaries . . . paraphrasing, summarizing [what] I read."

Andrew attended high school a quarter mile away from Bristol's Fall River campus, at Durfee High. He felt this helped him make the transition to college, because he was "more familiar with the teachers, the area, the resources at BCC." While a high school student, he wrote, in his words, a "fair amount," approximately eight papers per term, including papers in English courses as well as in his Portuguese history class. He also composed what he referred to as summaries of lab findings in science courses and papers for other history courses. He remembered one paper where he was allowed to select a specific time period to research; he selected the Revolutionary War, a current interest of his.

At the start of the fall semester, Andrew thought he'd be doing a "pretty good amount of writing, more than high school" while in college and getting better-quality feedback: "The writing is the same, but I would expect more critiquing; professors and teachers should

be more apt [*sic*] to correcting papers to strengthen writing skills."
He expected to do writing in all of his courses except algebra.

While not all incoming students have had experience incorpo-
rating research into their writing, Andrew seems fairly confident
about this task, considering such writing "easier" than other types.
Regarding what makes it easier, he explained, "You have more to
reflect upon than writing an essay or memoir or such . . . I can kind
of search on the Web site or books and pull certain pieces and turn
it into my own words." He recalled his high school history paper
on the Revolutionary War in some detail. His thesis had to do with
"the patriotism exerted by the citizens at that point, the farmers.
And defeating the redcoats toward the end of the war." When he
did his research, he was looking specifically for "the organization
that the Americans did at that point in time. How they banded
together to try and defeat the British, when they invaded America.
I kind of, I based it on the patriotism and how these farmers at that
time in history didn't want to take, I guess, orders if you will from
the British in England at that time because it almost seems like they
were a dictator, so many miles away, so I kind of based it on that
and how, how a small group of people banded together, worked very
well together and developed a strong alliance."

While he researched, he recorded "bullet points." He then "in
brief detail explain[ed] each bullet point, so instead of going back
to the resource and reading it all over again, I ha[d] the main parts
that I [was] going to work with on a piece of paper." Like many
students his age, Andrew turned to the Internet to find sources: "It
had all different kinds of history websites, and I did ask my teacher
for advice on what websites to turn to, to research, but for the most
part, I'd use the Internet."

This piece focuses not on the "how," but the "why," on one of the
causes of the colonists' rebellion, the tea tax:

> Americans were still outraged about the Tea Tax because they
> were major consumers of tea and didn't believe they were obli-
> gated to the pay the tax [*sic*]. The tea on tax [*sic*] was intended
> to stop other European [*sic*] from trading with the colonies
> and was also intended to stop competition within the indus-

try. England enforced this tax to prevent the closing of their own company, the British East India Tea Company. Well, the colonies would have none of this and decided to take matters into their own hands.

The other history paper is also an informative piece, this time a biographical sketch. He was asked to compose a "brief biography (role in American Revolution) of a personality on either side in the American Revolutionary War." Andrew made a logical, if safe, choice of topic, one he had begun to explore previous to this assignment and had genuine interest in, and one that is sure to have ample available resources, George Washington. He writes, "George Washington started his military career early on in life after the deaths of his father and half-brothers. At the ripe age of 22 he escalated through military ranks with a promotion to Lieutenant Colonel after he had become an adjutant of one of Virginia's four military districts. This important role caused him to be dispatched by Gov. Robert Dinwiddie to warn the French of future consequences if they continued disrupting British lands."

Although Andrew said he conducted and drew heavily upon research, citations were absent from his paper, despite being a requirement of the assignment. Guidelines for the assignment—at least those reproduced for our viewing in Andrew's notes—were limited: "Choose one of the following [five topics]. The essays you write this semester will count as ¼ of the semester grade. The three tests will count ¾. I expect one to two pages (maximum) with some references cited (text-website etc)." We might expect the lack of citations given Andrew's past experience with "Internet research," likely cutting and pasting relevant information without attribution—and with the best of intentions. He simply continued to use techniques that had worked for him in the past. Although he enjoyed reflective assignments, neither history paper showed Andrew challenging or complicating the "facts," events, or causal sequencing uncovered in his research.

In describing his writing process, Andrew mentioned brainstorming as the first task, something he does for a "few minutes" as soon as he receives an assignment. This doesn't involve putting pen to paper or finger to keyboard, however: "without writing it down, I kind of brainstorm in my head . . . [to] pull out all the ideas."

When he has selected the ideas he likes best, he begins writing: "I write up a draft. I take a look at the draft, [which] could be a couple of pages long. If I have to shorten it, I shorten it or if I have to lengthen it, I'll do that too." The draft is composed linearly, beginning with the introductory paragraph after he records his bullet points and main theme. He doesn't mention conducting research as part of the process, though he reveals in multiple conversations that this is a fairly common jumping-off point for his papers.

Once he has a draft completed, he does some revising himself and then seeks advice from others, particularly the person who assigned the writing: "I read it over. I, if I get a chance to, I will bring it to the teacher. Most times it doesn't happen only because I'm short on time or I don't have time to visit the teacher. So I will, once I'm done with the draft, read it over maybe once or twice or three times. If I like it, I'll keep it that way. Ninety percent of the time, I will change things here and there." When he does make changes, he explains, they mainly have to do with validating information, checking paragraph and sentence structure, and "rearrang[ing]" wording to "make it fit."

As a college student, Andrew began to seek feedback from people besides his instructors. In his college writing class, for example, he participated in peer review but still prefers to hear what his professor has to say: "I guess it's kind of good to get the same or similar perspective from a person my age and what changes they think I should do to the paper, but I do like to hear more from the teacher since they have the experience and knowledge." His perception that the professor's feedback is more useful than that of peers hadn't changed by the end of his first semester: the instructor has "a Ph.D. in the subject, so he knows a lot more than I do, but as far as my peers go, I think that most of the time they respond different to my essays, and I get different types of negative feedback like, 'Maybe you could have done a little bit more research on this part,' or 'You could have answered that question more,' which is understandable because sometimes they have less knowledge of the subject than I do." His reaction to peer review suggests that Andrew was developing a sense of audience.

Like Kim, Andrew seemed to be learning that his professors—and other readers—expect different things from his writing: "everyone's got their own style of writing, and some people are narrow minded and that's not necessarily a bad thing. They're just used to their own style. They haven't been introduced to other styles of writing that other people are used to, and I think that when you receive feedback whether it's from a teacher, a relative, a student, that it really opens up other pathways as to certain styles you could use for writing."

Andrew believed his English instructor offered more "critical" feedback on his writing than did his other professors: "His comments . . . I never know what he's going to say because the subject always differs, whether it's an argumentative essay or the film review or the scholarly article essay. Everything, it's always different subjects. I never know what he's going to say, and I take his comments seriously." Here he was referring to comments that responded directly to the ideas he'd presented, not in a generic or "stamped" format. He preferred such a response because "not every piece of work is the same. They're all different and [my English instructor] kind of tunes his focus into that particular piece of work, and kind of picks out what should or shouldn't belong in that type of writing, in that genre."

Though he felt he had received ample writing instruction, at least in his College Writing course, during his first semester at college, Andrew's writing process had changed only slightly by week fourteen: "I'm more sensitive to the word choice I put into the essays. Like before I would [write], I took time to actually understand what I was writing. I just picked out vocabulary. But this time when I actually sit down and even before . . . I guess before I actually write my rough draft, I actually consider words or which pieces or which sentences, paragraphs, words [to use], so that's definitely a change for me."

By the end of the fall semester, Andrew reported having done a "good amount" of writing, mainly in his writing course. One thing that seemed to surprise him about the writing he was asked to do in this course was the different types of writing assigned. While he expected feedback to differ from what he'd received in high school, he hadn't anticipated being asked to compose in new forms: "I've never written a detailed argumentative essay, and the film review was new to me, so that type of writing when going, just writing or paraphrasing or summarizing something that I read in high school opposed to actually analyzing, critically analyzing a certain piece in college wasn't difficult for me. It was new . . . kind of . . . a bump in the road, but it wasn't too difficult to form because I took the advice that I received."

In high school he was used to summarizing textbook reading, while in college he had been asked to respond to different types of texts. To explain, he offered the example of the assignment in English that required him to respond to a scholarly essay: "With the scholarly essay, you have experts in the field that are writing the pieces. You have a point of view from different people who are offering their opinion on the issue, so you actually have to kind of take apart the points."

Another new form was the film review:

I learned in English how to write a film review, which was the first time I had ever written one. I've never done it before. It was new to me. It was kind of a learning experience because my first draft wasn't that great. . . . I don't think that I'll be asked to write a film review, but I think it's good knowledge to have. And again, I didn't really have much interest because normally you go to a movie and you go there to sit down and relax and watch the film, and now I was asked to analyze it, which was something I had never done before, so I actually had to go to different websites to see how they actually layout the format of writing a review, which again was new to me.

The argumentative essay on the war in Iraq, a topic no doubt selected due to his brother's recent service as a U.S. Marine in Iraq, was the piece he enjoyed the most: "I think I wrote it with a lot of passion because my major is political science anyway and the war interests me a lot. . . . I have relatives that are over there serving now. . . . I didn't have to do too much research because I have a pretty good amount of knowledge on it, just from listening to the news and doing my own research prior to this." Andrew's positive assessment of this paper seemed influenced by his instructor's comments. Andrew noted two of them: "You are informed, persuasive, and eloquent" and "I was especially eager to see how you would present the other side." He concluded, "So, in my opinion, this was my strongest writing essay." The instructor's comments on this piece were limited, which Andrew found surprising: "I was kind of taken back by that . . . and he said, 'Other than this slight modification that you could have made' . . . But it wasn't necessary. The entire essay was good." Andrew embraced the positive feedback from a valued source.

Writing in new forms in this English course posed a welcomed challenge for Andrew. He struggled to understand the components of one genre in particular, the film review. While he had experience with narrative that could be drawn upon for the memoir and was able to present an argument (drawing upon Internet-based research) in his editorial, he admitted he wasn't familiar with the film review and turned to the Internet for help: "I actually had to go to different Web sites to see how they actually lay out the format of writing a review, which again was new to me." This search for samples of the genre included a search specifically for others' reviews of the movie he'd selected: "I formed my own perspective. I mean, I think I read three or four different reviews before I went to watch it, and there were certain parts of the movie where each review has different perspectives, different views. And I guess I kind of formed my own perspective and took pieces of each one." This search began after being given a detailed assignment that identified the required components, including a response to "opposing views." Asked to provide "clear and precise reasons" and "acknowledgment of opposing views," he turned to secondary source material, perhaps feeling shaky in his own abilities to analyze the primary text. Though Andrew liked being asked for his reaction, he was hesitant about offering it without first testing the water. He preferred to have some context—a framework on which to build his own understanding. In his review, such analysis was limited to his final paragraph, the remainder of the piece tracing some of the "thumbs up" and "thumbs down" responses to aspects of the film such as character development:

> While I do have to agree that there are some good observations on those who both liked and disliked the film, I would recommend this film to anyone who loves action, thrills, and suspense. There are many, in my opinion, characteristics that make this movie really interesting to watch. For one, it has a great cast and talented groups of actors and it also has a believable story line. Not that it's very likely anything like this would happen, it shows the possibility as well as some insight on how corrupt any government can be. It takes a certain level of corruption to protect freedom. That may be unfortunate, but it's the truth. So is this movie really worth the $10.00 dollars to see? Absolutely! I would recommend it to anyone. "Shooter" definitely earns a spot in my top 10 favorite movies.

Although Andrew had difficulty with this piece, he admitted that the struggle resulted in a valuable educational experience, saying, "I think that was probably one of the biggest learning experiences that I've had in that class." He elaborated, "The biggest learning experiences that I've had have been in English. For the most part the writing I've had in history, I've done similar writing in high school, so it hasn't really been new to me. I've kind of grown accustomed to it." This course required writing seven papers in total, including an in-class essay, a midsemester self-reflective progress report, and trend analysis in addition to those already discussed. Andrew was engaged by writing when it allowed him to discover different uses for writing and different rhetorical strategies to achieve those ends. Pushed to take some calculated risks, he did so with the safety net he'd woven, its threads consisting of instructor guidance/feedback and Web-accessible resources.

5

Implications for Teaching and Research

DESIGNING ASSIGNMENTS

WHEN WE BEGAN THIS STUDY, we hypothesized that faculty at our college were assigning writing in classes other than the first-year required English courses and that writing assignments would reflect the complex mission of the college, promoting both academic and workplace literacy. Our work in the multidisciplinary writing center provided some basis for our assumptions: while the majority of the writing that tutors see in the center comes from English courses, roughly 40 percent comes from social sciences, most conspicuously criminal justice, history, human services, and psychology. Writing comes as well from dental hygiene, biology, and art. We need to keep in mind, however, that the writing center serves students well beyond their first semester—which, of course, is our focus in this study. A study of our cohort portfolios strongly supports the perception that a preponderance of writing done in that first semester occurs in the required English courses only.

That fact has implications for our second hypothesis in that the writing done in English courses favors the essay over other forms of composition—a genre that, for all intents and purposes, lives mostly in the classroom and not in the workplace. We conclude that what David Russell calls the "myth of transience" is alive and well at Bristol: in other words, the idea that writing instruction in an English course transfers easily to writing done in any course (Russell 3). "Talking with the pen or keyboard," as it were, calls for the same set of skills whatever the discipline or course or genre. But, as with the mission of the community college itself, our assessment of these matters is complex and dialogic. Writing assignments that emerge from the college's career areas strongly suggest a workplace-specific set of criteria. We point, for example, to an interview assignment in occupational therapy (showcased in chapter 3), for which students need to "integrate relevant academic knowledge through case study" and demonstrate "skills of self awareness, listening, and therapeutic communication." While occupational therapy can hardly claim a monopoly on the importance of listening skills, this assignment has moved well beyond assessing written performance on the basis of paragraph logic or clarity of thesis—conventional markers of the academic essay. Rather, students are asked, as part of their assignment, to do what is expected at the job and to report on whether they have met expectations. The same can be said of communication students, who are asked by their instructor to compose a "feature news story" for the college newspaper. Students need not only to be able to conduct an interview effectively, they need to demonstrate a knowledge of the news story genre, which, while sharing similarities with the essay, is also distinctively different (especially in its attention to capturing an urgency and immediacy as expressed in speech and described behavior).

Students will achieve little, of course, unless the assignments provide the opportunity for engagement and growth. "Given the right conditions," asserts George Hillocks, "nearly all students can become engaged" (21). What are those conditions? Put another way, what features must an effective assignment have? Conversely, what flaws in assignment design prevent student engagement and development? Guided by our study and our years of work in the writing center, we offer these characteristics as essential to effective design of assignments for our students:

1. *Show students what success looks like.* Many of our students have never seen some of the forms of writing required in college and would benefit by seeing genres "in action." What, for example, does an annotated bibliography look like? When Andrew, a student in our cohort, was asked to write a film review, he had had little exposure to the genre. He became familiar with the genre by seeking out examples.

2. *Spell out criteria for success.* Many of our students have sufficient motive to succeed but need directions on the road. Many also
lack a vocabulary and metaknowledge for talking about successful
writing. What makes for an effective piece of college-level writing?
Or as Kim, one of our cohort asked of her English instructor, What
constitutes a "perfect paper"?

3. *Suggest processes for succeeding.* More than one of our students
commented on what they saw as a key difference between high school
and college—at least in regards to writing instruction in English
courses. In high school, they assert, a task would be given but with
little direction as to how to achieve it. In college, they claim, students are shown not only what they are to produce but how to go
about doing it. Realizing that it is hardly fair to generalize on all
writing instruction—at either the high school or college level—we
take the point seriously nonetheless: process matters. Students need
to be shown how to go about achieving success: what steps ought
to be taken?

4. *Develop incremental stages for complex writing tasks.* Imagine
being asked, as Kim and her fellow students were, to write an "autobiography" in your general psychology course in which you apply
the theories of Erickson and Maslow. Left to your own devices to
complete the assignment, you might be tempted to begin with what
you know best: your own story. And so you tell your story, compel-
ling as it is. But you lose sight of the second half of the assignment: to
theorize your account through the lens of Erickson and Maslow. You
attempt to jury rig the theory to your narrative but end up adding a
new and somewhat disconnected section to your paper. How might
this have been avoided? An assignment divided into several stages
might have prevented this problem: the student could have been
asked to engage the theories initially through a summary exercise.
She might then have been asked to synthesize her sources: where
are the overlaps? Where do they differ? These steps could have been
followed with the beginning of an analysis, stipulating a hypothesis
that could enable her to manage her own life story.

5. *Allow for formative and substantive feedback.* Student after student in our project called upon faculty to provide guidance through

their written feedback, feedback that could then be employed to improve their writing. While our access to faculty commentary was limited, what we saw in cohort portfolios provided important lessons: private notes or check marks (whose meaning is known only by the faculty member) do little to promote student learning. Feedback that is not grounded in the assignment criteria does nothing but confuse the student and further reinforces perceptions of faculty bias and subjectivity. The most useful feedback was rooted in clearly and explicitly stated criteria. In addition, we noted the facilitative nature of effective commentary, affirming what Knoblauch and Brannon (over two decades ago) called the "writer's on-going pursuit of meanings" (130).

6. *Provide ample opportunities for drafting.* Another clear difference between high school and college writing instruction, our students claimed, was the sheer amount of revision expected in college (at least in the first semester). We were impressed by our students' willingness to allow their writing to go through several drafts in response to faculty feedback. While in some cases the revision seemed nothing more than attending to localized editing matters (to move a grade from A- to A), in other situations students engaged in changing global features of their writing, such as gaps in logic or the lack of grounding detail. As a group, our students were more than willing to undertake significant changes to their work. Shall we not give them the opportunity to do so?

RESPONDING TO STUDENT WRITING: WRITING FOR OUR AUDIENCE

We need to look at our students' writing and ask to what extent and in what ways it has improved as a result of our teaching. There is no reason that most students should not show improvement. If they do not, the teaching needs to change. (Hillocks 207)

We rhetoricians remind our students that their writing will be read, so they should keep purpose and audience in mind. While we admit to the constraints of our study and thus to the problems of generalizing from a limited sample, a review of students' portfolios in this study reveals that we may not be practicing what we preach. Too often our written comments fail to relate directly back to the criteria stipulated within the assignment. Perhaps it is the sheer volume of papers we must read that causes us, at times, to offer patterned responses or generalized mandates such as "Nice detail!" and "Don't include new ideas in your conclusion." The comments collected indicate that our student writers don't always know what we think about what they wrote. And our conversations with them made it clear that they surely want to know the extent to which they've met our expectations. They also want to know what we think about their ideas.

Whatever the reason for limited response, students are disappointed by it. They are also confused by feedback that doesn't seem to consider the context in which the piece was written, particularly the specific instructions laid out in the assignment. Such feedback suggests to students that there is a hidden agenda. Finally, students want us to do more than identify errors; if we find problems, they want to know why or how what they've done is an issue. Too often, it seems, we make assumptions about students' past experiences with writing—and learning—making false assumptions about our readers that cause us to compose comments that are interpreted in ways we didn't intend. Worse yet, despite an awareness of ineffectual comments, we continue on in the same manner, failing to listen to our audience.

Tina, Kim, Nicole, and others reacted with frustration to the feedback of at least one of their professors. The source of this frustration was often a lack of clarity, particularly in terms of a disjuncture between the guidelines offered, the task itself, and what the instructor seemed to be emphasizing when responding to a draft.

RESPONSE STRATEGIES OF NON-ENGLISH FACULTY

A careful review of portfolios of students in the study reveals that faculty in disciplines other than English offer fewer comments on student writing. While nearly every paper written for a section of basic or college writing included marginal, in-text, and summative comments, this wasn't the case with papers written in courses such as psychology, chemistry, economics, or history. Some students seemed to expect this disparity, like Ben, who thought it wasn't the job of his marketing instructor to teach English: "the paper where I got lots of 'Very goods' [next to] every paragraph was my marketing class, so she's not going to go into an explanation that you did a very good job explaining why you want this because it's not really—her job as a marketing teacher isn't to teach me English. That's my English teacher's job." This isn't, of course, a perception we'd like to foster. Reactions like Nicole's, expressing her frustration at the single comment on the bibliography written for her management course, don't seem as typical.

Another student's nine-page history paper titled "Hatchepsut and Her Life Accomplishments" received a grade and a single written comment, "Good Work." One student's chemistry lab report was returned with comments that conveyed annoyance: "I asked you not to just say that your unknown had the same characteristics as one of the knowns! Describe what you saw!"

Such variance is likely what causes students to perceive that their instructors are all looking for very different things in their writing. The reality is that checks, hyphens, and lack of comments don't help students understand what is expected by their instructors, or within the genres and disciplines in which they're writing.

We note as well that responses in non-English courses seemed to focus more on correctness than on students' ideas. Some of the counter examples involved journal assignments in a psychology course. In one such entry, for example, Tina began, "The term 'normal' means when you don't have anything wrong with you, such as having a disorder or disability of any kind, looking or talking different." Circling the word "different," her instructor asked in the margin, "Who defines what's 'different?'" Such lines of questioning didn't, however, have any overt implications for Tina's future entries. The inquiry seemed to be quickly forgotten.

INSTRUCTOR RESPONSE IN BASIC AND COLLEGE WRITING COURSES

While in English courses writing instructors' responses seemed more engaged with student ideas than those of colleagues in other disciplines, such comments were far fewer in number than those indicating grammatical, syntactic, or mechanical issues. Some made syntactic observations, some circled each and every spelling error, and some identified every personal pronoun. A number of faculty not only identified what they considered ineffective phrasing but also struck out the phrase and wrote what they thought was a more effective phrase atop it. Some faculty focused on a single feature or two through a progression of drafts while others addressed a new "issue" with each draft. Modeling was quite common. Summative comments were often found at the end of students' papers, but not always. It was common to find an encouraging statement at the end of the paper (for example, "This is a very good essay"), but it was equally likely to find positive comments in the margins as well. Only occasionally were there references made to future drafts.

Checkmarks, dashes, and circled paragraphs were identified by some of the students in the study as vague or confusing. Although Haswell advocates "minimal marking," he recommends a two-step process ("Complexities" 19). What may well be happening in these cases is that the second step, namely for students to have their subsequent corrections evaluated by the instructor, is being omitted.

In one case, a student wasn't sure why her instructor had highlighted certain phrases and sections of her papers. Instead of seeking clarification, she did her best to guess what was meant. These guesses may have been misguided: "That might mean like different things should be rearranged and, just like the wording is in it." When asked whether she could be wrong, she replied, "I could be wrong. I'm assuming that's what it means." She admitted that she hadn't asked her instructor directly for clarification, and she didn't seem to have any intentions of doing so.

An assessment of the feedback offered within these portfolios might properly involve students' response to that feedback. Such response is manifest in subsequent drafts, though we also can draw upon our conversations with students about the feedback process.

Did professors' responses to student writing provoke further engagement with the material discussed? One way to answer this question is to consider whether students were sufficiently engaged to feel a significant connection to, and pride in, their work. When offered the opportunity to revise after submitting a paper to their instructor, students generally made only those changes suggested. Though this is in part a learned reaction, an idea we'll discuss momentarily, such a reflex wasn't discouraged by the responses offered. In other words, instructors' responses didn't explicitly or implicitly encourage students to make changes other than those suggested. Nancy Welch sees this as a problem:

> The students I've worked with don't always know how to take the next step of intervening in a draft's meanings and representations. Or, in the context of a composition classroom, they understand that "revision" means the very opposite of such work, the systematic suppression of all complexity and contradiction. Another problem: Composition teachers by and large haven't been asking questions like "Something missing, something else?" that promote revision as getting restless with familiar and constrictive ways of writing and being, as creating alternatives. We respond instead . . . in ways that restrict revision to a "narrowing" of focus, the correction of an "inappropriate tone" or "awkward repetition," the changing of any passage that might "confuse, mislead, or irritate" readers. (135–36)

She considers revision a negotiation as opposed to a constriction or ultimatum, allowing students to maintain a key role in the evolving texts. Beyond the idea of ownership, Welch argues for breaking out of patterns, for encouraging students to consider alternatives, to experiment with new ideas and ways of thinking and writing. We might expect students to feel unsettled when asked to consider what is missing, when asked "what else?" during the revision process, but this shift has strong possibilities to engage students if handled in a progressive, developmental manner. Again, such an enterprise requires regular writing and feedback.

While our interviews with students in the cohort indicate that they appreciate instructors who allow them to maintain ownership over their writing, when they believe the instructor is demanding certain changes, they are generally quick to oblige, as did Wendy with her "One Man's Junk" paper. When confronted with handwriting on their once-neat draft, emerging writers may feel compelled to surrender control, particularly in this situation where a presumed expert is acting as audience.

Students in the study, including those represented in the cases, seemed to reflect most fondly upon "pre-writing" activities, indicating the writer-based mode in which they were situated. This isn't surprising and may be a useful perception to draw upon when responding to student work. If students appreciate choice and the opportunity to sort things out, perhaps we should respond in a manner that allows them to continue to do so through the revision process. In other words, we should be less quick to encourage "clean up," instead accepting and encouraging dissonance—complication, contradiction, and confusion—while resisting the urge to sort things out for students. This process would require multiple drafts and a significant time commitment on the part of already overworked faculty. Currently, students are allowed to revise their work mainly in their English courses and even there on a limited basis. If it is important for us to encourage our students to think critically, we must overcome this obstacle.

The students in our cohort, when asked what kind of feedback they found most useful, pointed to this kind of response, although they also appreciated less open-endedness, more direction. One student liked "kicks" that helped her think about developing an idea. Another preferred comments that asked her to develop ideas further. Kim may have been the most outspoken about the guidance she sought, explaining that she appreciated feedback that let her know that her writing wasn't "junk," that there was something with which to work. She thought the best comments provided a "path," a "direction to follow," but allowed her to choose which way to go.

While it is tempting to establish a hierarchy of effective commenting methods, perhaps with a solitary grade at one end and dialogic, open-ended response at the other, our students seemed to struggle with both extremes. Tina, for example, had unlimited opportunities for revision and extensive questions and suggestions in her basic writing course, starting with the first assignment and carrying through to the last. The mode of feedback remained un-changed, with the exception of a reduction in marginal comments and references to past drafts and advice for later papers. This static feedback approach didn't work for Tina, who had learned, in high school, to expect directive comments and explicit corrections on her first draft. Without such a firm voice, Tina was forced to assume control of her work while working toward a more reader-centered agenda; the problem was that she wasn't provided with a sufficient transition between the significantly different forms of response. Her response was to resist suggestions, repeatedly throwing her hands up in frustration, unable to reenvision her work or to accept the idea that her paper might evolve beyond a first-draft, final-draft sequence. Instead of deeply appreciating that her instructor was encouraging her to own her work, to make her own decisions, Tina wanted to be told what to "fix."

This makes sense given Haswell's review of the literature on re-sponse: students "don't consume teacher response very well." He explains further that although "students are avid for commentary . . . they misinterpret a shocking portion of it." When students do revise, as in Tina's case, "they assiduously follow the teacher's surface emendations and disregard the deeper suggestions regarding content and argumentation. They prefer global, non-directive, and positive comments but make changes mainly to surface, directive, and nega-tive ones . . . they want lots and certain kinds of response, but have trouble doing much with what they ask for" ("Complexities" 8).

The assumption made about students like Tina is that they desire ownership of their writing, which isn't necessarily the case. They may not have been given such opportunities in the past and so may resist changes to a comfortable pattern. Others may be seeking to exert minimal effort. Both groups exhibit a passive attitude, developed in large part from past academic experiences where behavior stem-ming from such an attitude was reinforced. Is it possible to change this attitude, to foster active learners? This is certainly a challenging prospect. Teachers of writing can work toward this goal by help-ing students develop an appreciation for the value and power of language. If we wish to respond dialogically, we need to encourage students to accept their role as conversant, akin to getting tutees involved in a tutoring session, to help them to understand why they need to make choices and how important these decisions can be.

To help students transition from mostly directive feedback (for example, "Stay with graduation party for your conclusion") to mostly nondirective (for example, "I see that you don't bring up your graduation party here; I take this to mean that you want readers to know you've moved on"), particularly in the initial semester, it would be helpful for students to be faced with fewer choices, fewer nondirective comments initially. Perhaps more importantly, revisions made by students in response to nondirective comments should get special attention. This may involve noting the change, letting students know we are aware of the decision, and could involve mentioning the effect(s) of the change. Such reinforcement helps diminish anxiety students may feel about not choosing the "correct" response and thus not delivering what the instructor really wants. If nondirective comments are ignored, instructors may want to comment upon the result there as well, helping students see that these possibilities/issues remain and can eventually be tackled in future drafts. In other words, we can begin the semester by offering some practice with nondirective commenting for those students who aren't familiar or comfortable with this response strategy. Offering a truly developmental approach means, of course, that students will increase their comfort levels and revision skills at varying speeds. Setting an appropriate pace—of more choices and fewer directives—is a challenge. As a runner paces with a stopwatch, so must we use drafts to note changes in comfort and confidence of our student writers. Let's not expect six-minute miles during initial training runs.

If instructors wish to use their responses to prod students to take ownership of their writing and if they want to do so incrementally, they might consider that one or two writing assignments during the semester don't allow for such progression. Ungraded and/or informal pieces of writing could be added to allow for more development to take place.

Another way to think about the question of student engagement is to consider the extent to which faculty reacted to their ideas. A number of students in the study, a third of those who sat for the initial interview, thought that good writing kept the reader interested. Students may well gauge their success in this area by the types of comments they see on the papers returned to them. Few comments or comments that fail to take up the author's ideas may be read as disinterest and could cause the student author to put less time and effort into future work. Some students have arrived at college disengaged in terms of their writing, thinking that good writing is about correctness, in terms of both grammar and responding properly to the assigned prompt; it doesn't matter what they say, just how they say it.

To enhance the efficacy of our response, surely a worthwhile goal given the time we devote to reading and responding, we would do well to pay attention to what students do and don't do with our feedback. One-on-one conferences can help here. Meeting with students after the first set of papers is returned can help uncover how our comments have been interpreted, perhaps by asking them to explain concepts we've referred to in their own words. We can also discover what students' plans are for revising their work. How, for example, will they focus that third paragraph? Why are certain details irrelevant? What will it mean for them to clarify purpose? Such a conference provides an opportunity to push beyond the "it needs to flow better" avoidance maneuver toward more genuine communication. Encouraging students to voice confusion and to assert themselves in the face of expert advice will help them develop a more active mindset that will prove crucial in their literacy development.

IMPACT OF THE STUDY ON THE RESEARCHERS

Working so closely with these students yielded significant benefits, as we typically see our students only in groups of twenty-five or so with the understanding that they are there to earn college credits and/or a grade with which they'll be pleased. Not held to the confines of a semester time frame, we listened in on students' nervous anticipation of their first semester at college as well as the pride, frustration, understanding, and confusion occurring after grades had been recorded. They didn't have to stop by to see us, but they did, doing so at times that were meaningful to them. We were thus in a good position to assess the challenges faced by our students day to day, and, perhaps, helped by simply listening to their stories. We think it safe to say that as teacher/researchers we emerged from such conversations with a renewed respect for our students' resilience in the light of these challenges.

Yet we also come away with a sense of astonishment at the frenetic pace of our students' lives. It is surely no cliché to write that our students are always on their way to somewhere else and thus have little time, as we used to say, "to shoot the breeze." As we noted in an earlier chapter, staying in touch with the broader cohort (a group, originally, of over forty students) proved quite difficult. Indeed, getting a majority into a single room for a meeting proved impossible. No less challenging was arranging for this group to drop papers off for collection in a portfolio.

To complicate matters further, we had to help students understand our role as teacher-researchers, to break down layers of doubt that may have existed due to past educational experiences. Toward this end, we tried to be as transparent as possible, letting students know about our goals, plans, and our own frustrations and successes relative to this project, at regular intervals. We were always happy to see them, always eager to listen. And yet we cannot be altogether certain that all doubts about our role were resolved. After all, these were students who, by and large, had slipped under the radars of many teachers: how could these students be faulted for doubting that we two teachers could really take the time to know them? None need doubt, however, the impact of this project and these students on our own teaching.

UNINTENDED CONSEQUENCES OF THIS STUDY
Howard Tinberg

While I have remained committed to writing instruction in my own courses over the years, I have acknowledged often enough to myself and to colleagues in my department and beyond that writing instruction is a shared responsibility of all in the college who attend to student learning and development. In doing so, I have opted not to prepare students for the various writing tasks that await them elsewhere in the curriculum. After all, how much can be accomplished in a mere fifteen weeks and by someone whose expertise does not extend to writing in history, sociology, human services, or occupational therapy?

But my experience in this project has led me to an inescapable truth: that the most intense conversation about writing continues to take place in the required writing course. While significant writing opportunities beyond the English department are given to students (and we have noted many of them in this study), the depth of commitment to student writing (and therefore in writing instruction) is most obvious in the students' College Writing course than elsewhere. What does this fact mean for my own writing pedagogy? I wonder whether I need to revert to the view that colleagues in writing across the curriculum have been positing for decades: that my obligation to teach writing in our college writing course ought to extend to preparing students for academic writing beyond the first fifteen weeks of college. In other words, I should be preparing students to write and think in ways that are transferable to other academic subjects. Clearly, such a practice would, on one level, lend merit to the myth of transience mentioned earlier and absolve others from the heavy lifting of discussing what writing does in the disciplines while teaching those disciplines. Nevertheless, students need to receive the tools with which to succeed in writing tasks from somewhere. Rather than instruct my students for writing beyond the academy, as I have done in recent years (for example, writing a proposal or a news story or editorial), I wonder whether I should be preparing students for the intense work of analysis, synthesis, and argumentation, which conventionally form the backbone of academic discourse. When one of our cohort struggled mightily to synthesize theories of psychological development with her own life case (not receiving the instruction on how to do so in her psychology course), I could not help but think that little preparation for this kind of work would have been offered to her in my own course.

Jean-Paul Nadeau

Having had the time to talk with (and have lunch with—imagine!) student writers without having to eventually get into a discussion about grades, I am enthusiastic about continuing such student-centered learning and development in a classroom setting. While I have always been aware of the need to show enthusiasm for the material being discussed, I am currently striving to have each class meeting be less about me and more about students. By this I mean that I consciously try to get students involved on a more regular basis—and to resist the urge to jump in while a student is in midsentence. I am trying to continue to listen so that I don't return to making false assumptions about what my students already know and expect. The positive interactions I had with members of our cohort have even influenced the way in which I enter my own classrooms (with a smile and a "good morning/afternoon") and the way I (now enthusiastically) greet students arriving at my office. We now spend class time discussing students' understanding of terms they've been reading in the textbook, terms that may be used in ways different than they have in the past. I explain that this is a way for us to have a common language with which to analyze their writing, not a judgment of which definition is correct.

One of the many benefits of having done this research is that I've been able to share the results with my students. We've been able to have more engaging discussions about what it means to do research by examining Andrew's experiences, for example. Students have been eager to find out how much they should "be" in a research paper and how much research should be included. In other words, the students in the cohort have bravely begun the conversation, attempting to bridge a gap between student and faculty understanding of some challenging concepts, and my students are now able to cross sooner and more safely than was previously possible.

While I continue to revise my writing assignments based on students' responses, it is my feedback on student drafts that has been most influenced by this research. Long hours spent offering open-ended comments on drafts can easily seem futile when subsequent drafts provoke the same questions and lack of decisions on the part of the writer. My approach has become increasingly developmental, fine-tuned for individual students as I get to better understand them. Early in the semester I respond with more directive than nondirective comments, but gradually work to encourage more decision making on the part of the writer. My goal is to encourage students to make bold decisions by beginning with simpler choices. Once they see that their choices help the writing, they will be less worried about making the "wrong" choice (the option the teacher doesn't want them to make). The graduated nature of such response requires careful thought and time to craft, though my hope is that I'll get more efficient with practice.

PATHS FOR FUTURE RESEARCH

Student development, we acknowledge, cannot be traced in a narrowly defined study such as ours. We realize that in privileging the work of first-semester writers we can hardly make claims as to students' progress over time. While we continue to see the value of research that aims at first-semester community college students, we, frankly, hope to follow these students as they enter their second year of college work, whether at Bristol or elsewhere. Really, we want to watch for development, particularly in the way they respond to faculty expectations and the various obstacles confronting them. We urge others to follow this research path: studying community college writers over time and in context. In other words, we ask that a consideration of their work be seen not in isolation but within the complex matrix of faculty expectations (in many courses), the institutional mission (so often complex and comprehensive), and student aspirations (which can change over time).

A consideration of student writing must of necessity engage faculty response. While considerable research has been conducted over the last two decades on the nature and uses of faculty commentary, that research has focused primarily on the English classroom. Our study continues in that line, as most extensive written commentary on cohort writing appeared on work done in English. We see the need for additional research of faculty response in disciplines other than English (as called for by Haswell, "Complexities"). Writing centers may provide useful guidance here, in a variation of the "read around": in writing centers, useful discussion occurs when the staff reads student compositions. We see usefulness in faculty from across the curriculum doing similar reading, taking care to provide written commentary on selected writing samples.

Do faculty commentary and expectations at the community college reflect the mission and priorities of the institution? That is a key question raised by our study, one that we don't pretend to have definitively answered. After reviewing hours of conversations with faculty and students alike, we remain convinced that the question must be asked and answered. We surmise, based on our data, that just as the mission of the community college attempts to promote both academic and workplace literacies, so does writing instruction run the gamut as to what faculty expect from their community college students. In the career areas, we note an emphasis on what Michael Carter has referred to as "ways of doing" (388). In other words, students imbibe, through their writing assignments, a kind of procedural knowledge: how to do the work in the field. As we have seen, faculty may demonstrate the various steps needed to conduct interviews professionally or to create a lead to a news story and students are assessed in their ability to enact such practices. Those same faculty may insist on students' acquiring "ways of writing," in other words, a competence with the forms of written communication, including control of grammar and mechanics. That said, our study indicates, not surprisingly, that English faculty are more likely to promote such formal literacy than their colleagues elsewhere in the curriculum. The entire matter, however, remains unknowable and "academic" unless researchers take the time to study writing at the community college. We hope that our study can serve as a useful beginning and that, in future research, community college writers will be both honored and visible.

We would be remiss, however, if we limited our call for additional research of first-semester writers to community colleges. While we are committed to the distinctive mission of our particular institution and of the community college, we recognize, first and foremost, the preminent challenges represented by the first semester of college, regardless of whether that experience takes place in a two- or four-year college. All of us would benefit from taking the time to understand the pressures facing students new to college. At a time when a college education poses not only academic challenges but significant economic hurdles, we would all do well to ascertain the pressures faced by students who are no longer for the most part full-time students but rather students who work and attend school. We would also do well to consider and value (rather than merely critique) our students' urgent desire to put what they learn to practice beyond the classroom. We need not respond with binary thinking: students write for the academy in my class but write for the workplace in those other classes (perhaps at those other places, community and technical colleges). As we have learned in conversations with colleagues who teach in career-oriented fields, the work expected may be both academic- and career-relevant. Our study encourages us to think that both kinds of work are possible, just as it prompts us community college faculty to regard colleagues at four-year institutions as engaged in the same grand adventure: to enable students to meet the complex demands of twenty-first-century literacies.

APPENDIXES

WORKS CITED

INDEX

APPENDIX A: THE RESEARCH COHORT

Major		GPA
Business Admin. Transfer	Nicole	3.9
Health Science Option	Anne Marie	1.91
Business Admin. Transfer	Ben	3.39
Professional Option	Andrew	2.65
Health Science Option	Dilcelia	1.38
Business Admin. Transfer	Jane	3.36
Elementary Education	Tina	3.6
Nondegree	Wendy	4
Early Childhood Ed.	Katie	3.57
Health Science Option	Irma	2.9
Criminal Justice	Cathy	2.34
Business Admin. Career	Jo	2.18
Business Admin. Career	Frances	3.07
Communication	Lindsy	3.19
Humanities Option	Kim	3.92

APPENDIX B: THE STUDENT SURVEY

SURVEY OF FIRST-SEMESTER STUDENT WRITERS

This survey is part of a research project aimed at studying the "culture of writing" at a public community college. The project is funded by the Calderwood Writing Initiative at the Boston Athenaeum. We greatly appreciate your cooperation in completing this survey; be assured that information collected will be kept confidential and will be used for research purposes only.

Howard Tinberg, professor of English at Bristol
Community College in Massachusetts
J. P. Nadeau, instructor of English,
also at Bristol Community College

Age:_____ Gender:_____ Program/Major (e.g. Business Transfer):_____

In what year (e.g., 1984) did you graduate high school or earn your G.E.D.?
_____

Is English your first language? Please circle: Yes / No
Is this your first semester taking college courses for credit? (circle one)
Yes   No

Please indicate the extent to which you agree with the following statements using a scale of 1 to 5, 1 being "Strongly Disagree" and 5 being "Strongly Agree."

	Strongly Disagree	Disagree	Neutral	Agree	Strongly Agree
1. I expect to write regularly in college.	1	2	3	4	5
2. I am a strong writer.	1	2	3	4	5
3. Writing will be important in my career.	1	2	3	4	5
4. Writing well is an important skill for college students.	1	2	3	4	5

	Strongly Disagree	Disagree	Neutral	Agree	Strongly Agree

5. The last paper I wrote was successful.

| | 1 | 2 | 3 | 4 | 5 |

6. Writing is one of my strengths as a student.

| | 1 | 2 | 3 | 4 | 5 |

7. I can develop my writing skills.

| | 1 | 2 | 3 | 4 | 5 |

8. I seek out courses that require writing.

| | 1 | 2 | 3 | 4 | 5 |

9. I look forward to a challenging writing assignment.

| | 1 | 2 | 3 | 4 | 5 |

10. I avoid courses that require writing.

| | 1 | 2 | 3 | 4 | 5 |

11. Others' assessment of my writing matches my own.

| | 1 | 2 | 3 | 4 | 5 |

12. I begin working on a paper when it is assigned.

| | 1 | 2 | 3 | 4 | 5 |

13. Teacher feedback on my papers is helpful.

| | 1 | 2 | 3 | 4 | 5 |

14. I come up with ideas before beginning to write.

| | 1 | 2 | 3 | 4 | 5 |

15. I show my writing to someone before handing it to a teacher.

| | 1 | 2 | 3 | 4 | 5 |

16. I reread a paper before handing it in.

| | 1 | 2 | 3 | 4 | 5 |

17. I produce more than one draft before submitting a paper to my teacher.

| | 1 | 2 | 3 | 4 | 5 |

18. In my high school writing courses, I had to revise my work using classmates' feedback on drafts.

| | 1 | 2 | 3 | 4 | 5 |

19. The writing I'll do in college will be similar to the writing I've done in high school.

| | 1 | 2 | 3 | 4 | 5 |

20. In my high school writing courses, I had to revise my papers using teacher feedback on drafts.

| | 1 | 2 | 3 | 4 | 5 |

	Strongly Disagree	Disagree	Neutral	Agree	Strongly Agree

21. My high school writing teachers were more interested in my ideas than in my spelling, punctuation, and grammar.

| | 1 | 2 | 3 | 4 | 5 |

22. In my high school writing courses, I commented on other students' papers.

| | 1 | 2 | 3 | 4 | 5 |

23. In my high school writing courses, I spent time working in groups.

| | 1 | 2 | 3 | 4 | 5 |

24. My high school writing teachers were more interested in my spelling, punctuation, and grammar than in my ideas.

| | 1 | 2 | 3 | 4 | 5 |

25. Teacher feedback on my writing includes both negative and positive comments.

| | 1 | 2 | 3 | 4 | 5 |

26. My high school writing instruction prepared me to write papers in college.

| | 1 | 2 | 3 | 4 | 5 |

27. In high school I wrote papers using research.

| | 1 | 2 | 3 | 4 | 5 |

APPENDIX C: THE FACULTY SURVEY

SURVEY OF FACULTY AT BRISTOL
COMMUNITY COLLEGE
This survey is part of a research project aimed at studying what we're calling the "culture" of writing at BCC. We greatly appreciate your co-operation with our project, which is funded by the Calderwood Writing Initiative at the Boston Athenaeum. Information collected will be kept confidential and will be used for research purposes only.

Howard Tinberg and J. P. Nadeau

Please list the courses you teach:

_____

Are you a full-time faculty member?   Yes   No

Do you assign writing in one or more of your courses?
Yes   No

Please indicate the extent to which you agree with the following statements using a scale of 1 to 5, 1 being "Strongly Disagree" and 5 being "Strongly Agree."

	Strongly Disagree	Disagree	Neutral	Agree	Strongly Agree
1. Writing will be important in students' careers.					
	1	2	3	4	5
2. Writing well is an important skill for college students.					
	1	2	3	4	5
3. Students consider writing one of their strengths.					
	1	2	3	4	5
4. Students can develop their writing skills.					
	1	2	3	4	5
5. Students avoid courses that require writing.					
	1	2	3	4	5

	Strongly Disagree	Disagree	Neutral	Agree	Strongly Agree

6. Students begin working on a paper when it is assigned.

       1   2   3   4   5

7. The feedback I offer students on their papers is helpful.

       1   2   3   4   5

8. Students should brainstorm ideas before beginning to write.

       1   2   3   4   5

9. Before submitting a paper, students should bring a draft to the Writing Lab for review.

       1   2   3   4   5

10. Students should reread a paper before handing it in.

       1   2   3   4   5

11. I offer students feedback on their writing before conducting a final assessment.

       1   2   3   4   5

12. I expect students to produce multiple drafts of their work.

       1   2   3   4   5

13. Students benefit from receiving feedback before earning a grade for the paper.

       1   2   3   4   5

14. I conduct face-to-face conferences with students to discuss their writing in progress.

       1   2   3   4   5

15. I respond to student writing via electronic means.

       1   2   3   4   5

16. When grading student writing, I offer comments in the margins.

       1   2   3   4   5

17. When grading student writing, I offer a summative end comment.

       1   2   3   4   5

18. When grading student writing, I identify errors in spelling, grammar, word choice, and phrasing.

       1   2   3   4   5

19. I comment on student writing so students know why they earned the grade assigned.

       1   2   3   4   5

20. I comment on student writing so students can improve on the next paper.

       1   2   3   4   5

	Strongly Disagree	Disagree	Neutral	Agree	Strongly Agree

21. Students' writing improves as a result of the feedback I offer.

  1   2   3   4   5

22. Students are accustomed to producing multiple drafts of their writing.

  1   2   3   4   5

23. I expect my students to write papers using research.

  1   2   3   4   5

24. I discuss one or more elements of the writing process with students individually or as a class.

  1   2   3   4   5

25. Students focus too much on grammar and mechanics when revising their work.

  1   2   3   4   5

26. Students focus too much on logic and structure when revising their work.

  1   2   3   4   5

27. My writing assignments prove challenging for students.

  1   2   3   4   5

28. My students are well-prepared for challenging writing assignments at the start of the course.

  1   2   3   4   5

29. My students are well-prepared for challenging writing assignments at the end of the course.

  1   2   3   4   5

30. I require that my students write in-class essays rather than writing done outside of class.

  1   2   3   4   5

31. I require students to respond to objective questions on exams rather than short answer or essay questions.

  1   2   3   4   5

Additional Comments:

_____

_____

_____

_____

_____

_____

APPENDIX D: FACULTY INTERVIEW QUESTIONS

FACULTY INTERVIEW QUESTIONS

1. What brought you to BCC? What courses do you teach at BCC? How many sections?

2. Do you assign writing in these courses? If so, what kinds?

3. What are your students' attitudes (and perceptions) about writing, particularly the writing they are asked to do in your course(s)? If you could change one thing about students' attitudes about writing in your course(s), what would it be?

4. What do you expect of your students' writing? What elements make for an effective paper in your discipline?

5. Do you talk about the process of writing with students as a class or individually? Why/why not? If so, what aspects do you focus on?

6. Do students benefit from producing multiple drafts of their work? Is it beneficial for students to get feedback on a draft before it is submitted for a grade? Do you encourage your students to use the Writing Lab? Why/why not?

7. What generalizations can you draw about the writing students do in your courses (perhaps from the last set of papers you graded/read)? What do you find to be the biggest stumbling block student writers face? How would you describe first-semester BCC students' level of preparedness for college-level writing?

8. What is your method of responding to student writing? What is your motive when commenting on student writing? At what stage(s) do you see your students' writing? How is students' future writing affected by your responses?

9. What is your most challenging writing assignment, and why? Are students up to the challenge? Which assignment have you had the most success with and why?

APPENDIX E: STUDENT INTERVIEW QUESTIONS

INTERVIEW #1: QUESTIONS FOR
STUDENTS — SEPTEMBER 2007

1. How would you describe your writing ability?

2. How much writing, and what kinds of writing, did you do in high school?

3. How much writing, and what kinds of writing, do you expect you'll be given as a student at BCC?

4. Have you written papers using research? How would you describe what it was like writing with research? If you haven't written with sources, how do you feel about the idea of doing so?

5. What makes a paper effective?

6. How do you go about writing? Please describe your writing process.

7. What is the most useful response from a teacher that you have ever received on your writing?

INTERVIEW #2: QUESTIONS FOR
STUDENTS — NOVEMBER 2007

1. How much writing and what kinds of writing have you done so far this semester (in all classes)?

2. Which of your writing assignments did you enjoy (benefit from? excel at?) the most and why?

3. In which of your classes did you learn from the writing you did?

4. Have your writing abilities improved during the last 9 weeks? How so/not?

5. Has your writing process changed over the last 9 weeks? How/how not? (getting started, generating ideas, selection, organization, sentence crafting, revision, editing/proofreading, seeking feedback)

6. As you look back at your teachers' comments on your writing so far, how would you characterize those comments? In other words, what aspects of your writing have teachers focused on?

7. Have you had any surprises (pleasant or not) in terms of advice offered by faculty in terms of writing (e.g. is the 5x5 method dead)?

8. Is there a difference between the way your high school teachers and college professors responded to your writing?

APPENDIX F: STUDENT SURVEY RESULTS

Table: Survey Data
Key: B = Bristol (N = 339), PC = Participating Colleges (N = 1104)
Participating Colleges included Santa Barbara, Illinois Central, and Whatcom
SD = Strongly Disagree, D = Disagree, N = Neutral, A = Agree, SA = Strongly Agree
(Data represented as percentages)

	SD		D		N		A		SA
B	**PC**	**B**	**PC**	**B**	**PC**	**B**	**PC**	**B**	**PC**
1. I expect to write regularly in college.									
.9	.1	2.7	.8	11.2	8.2	49.7	46.9	35.2	44.1
2. I am a strong writer.									
6	3.4	19	15.6	45.8	46	24.1	28.3	4.5	5.8
3. Writing will be important in my career.									
1.5	1.1	11.6	9	34.6	37.6	37.3	34.2	14.6	17.5
4. Writing well is an important skill for college students.									
.3	.2	0	.5	7.5	4.3	41.9	38.1	50.3	56.6
5. The last paper I wrote was successful.									
1.8	1.5	6.3	6.4	32.4	26.4	44.6	45.7	14.9	19.9
6. Writing is one of my strengths as a student.									
8.4	7	24.2	21.7	38.5	35.7	22.1	27.8	6	7.3
7. I can develop my writing skills.									
.6	0	2.4	2.1	15.5	12.8	59.5	51.5	21.7	33.3
8. I seek out courses that require writing.									
9.3	7.9	29.4	30.7	42.9	41.6	15.3	15.5	3	4.2
9. I look forward to a challenging writing assignment.									
14.6	11.8	21.4	24.4	39.6	36.6	17.9	21.5	6.3	5.1
10. I avoid courses that require writing.									
18.1	18.2	43	39.8	30.9	31.8	5.6	7.9	1.5	1.9
11. Others' assessment of my writing matches my own.									
3.3	1.2	9	10.9	65.7	62.8	20.2	23.1	1.5	1.8
12. I begin working on a paper when it is assigned.									
2.7	4.4	19.2	20.8	29.3	31.3	38.8	34.1	10.1	9
13. Teacher feedback on my papers is helpful.									
.6	.1	.9	.8	4.4	4.9	43.8	35.6	50.3	58.2
14. I come up with ideas before beginning to write.									
.6	.6	5.3	4.9	19.2	17.7	47.3	51.1	27.5	25.5

	SD		D		N		A		SA	
	B	PC	B	PC	B	PC	B	PC	B	PC

15. I show my writing to someone before handing it to a teacher.

| | 4.5 | 4.1 | 22.6 | 18.6 | 29.2 | 30.6 | 33 | 30.2 | 10.7 | 16.2 |

16. I reread a paper before handing it in.

| | .9 | .5 | 3.9 | 3.6 | 8.6 | 12.4 | 51.2 | 43.9 | 34.8 | 39.6 |

17. I produce more than one draft before submitting a paper to my teacher.

| | 1.2 | 1.5 | 14 | 12.1 | 29.2 | 29.1 | 37.7 | 37.1 | 17.9 | 20.1 |

18. In my high school writing courses, I had to revise my work using classmates' feedback on drafts.

| | 5.4 | 3.9 | 21.7 | 13 | 23.8 | 19.9 | 36 | 43.6 | 12.8 | 19.3 |

19. The writing I'll do in college will be similar to the writing I've done in high school.

| | 5.4 | 3.9 | 21.4 | 21.9 | 44.6 | 38.6 | 25.3 | 31.1 | 3.3 | 3.5 |

20. In my high school writing courses, I had to revise my work using teacher feedback on drafts.

| | .9 | 1.8 | 6.3 | 6.5 | 17.9 | 20.1 | 56.8 | 51.7 | 17.6 | 19.5 |

21. My high school teachers were more interested in my ideas than in my spelling, punctuation, and grammar.

| | 6.8 | 8 | 23.8 | 24.9 | 37.2 | 34.5 | 24.4 | 23.7 | 7.7 | 8.4 |

22. In my high school writing courses, I commented on other students' papers.

| | 4.8 | 4.1 | 26.2 | 14.9 | 30.4 | 21 | 30.4 | 47.6 | 8.3 | 12.3 |

23. In my high school writing courses, I spent time working in groups.

| | 4.5 | 5 | 16.3 | 18.4 | 32.5 | 24.7 | 40.4 | 41.3 | 6.3 | 10.6 |

24. My high school writing teachers were more interested in my spelling, punctuation, and grammar than in my ideas.

| | 3 | 5.5 | 23.3 | 26.2 | 48.4 | 39.6 | 15.8 | 20.2 | 9.3 | 8.1 |

25. Teacher feedback on my writing includes both negative and positive comments.

| | .6 | .7 | 2.1 | 1.9 | 13.1 | 13.8 | 62.4 | 53.6 | 21.8 | 30.1 |

26. My high school writing instruction prepared me to write papers in college.

| | 4.2 | 3.9 | 9.2 | 8.1 | 26.8 | 31.4 | 47.6 | 39.7 | 12.2 | 16.4 |

27. In high school I wrote papers using research.

| | 2.7 | .9 | 4.2 | 4.4 | 18.5 | 15.4 | 49.7 | 50.7 | 25 | 28.3 |

APPENDIX G: FACULTY SURVEY RESULTS

Faculty Survey (N = 70)
SD = strongly disagree, D = disagree, N = neutral, A = agree, SA = strongly agree

	SD	D	N	A	SA
1. Writing will be important in students' careers.					
	1%	1%	3%	19%	76%
2. Writing well is an important skill for college students.					
	1%	0%	1%	10%	87%
3. Students consider writing one of their strengths.					
	9%	69%	18%	4%	0%
4. Students can develop their writing skills.					
	1%	3%	6%	26%	64%
5. Students avoid courses that require writing.					
	1%	10%	31%	39%	19%
6. Students begin working on a paper when it is assigned.					
	32%	51%	10%	3%	3%
7. The feedback I offer students on their papers is helpful.					
	0%	4%	14%	59%	22%
8. Students should brainstorm ideas before beginning to write.					
	0%	0%	4%	47%	49%
9. Before submitting a paper, students should bring a draft to the Writing Lab for review.					
	1%	3%	22%	45%	29%
10. Students should reread a paper before handing it in.					
	0%	0%	0%	11%	89%
11. I offer students feedback on their writing before conducting a final assessment.					
	4%	9%	21%	42%	24%
12. I expect students to produce multiple drafts of their work.					
	8%	23%	30%	23%	17%
13. Students benefit from receiving feedback before earning a grade for the paper.					
	0%	4%	10%	43%	42%
14. I conduct face-to-face conferences with students to discuss their writing in progress.					
	3%	16%	38%	28%	15%
15. I respond to student writing via electronic means.					
	13%	21%	13%	37%	16%

	SD	D	N	A	SA

16. When grading student writing, I offer comments in the margins.

	0%	0%	7%	42%	51%

17. When grading student writing, I offer a summative end comment.

	0%	6%	25%	28%	41%

18. When grading student writing, I identify errors in spelling, grammar, word choice, and phrasing.

	0%	2%	2%	42%	55%

19. I comment on student writing so students know why they earned the grade assigned.

	0%	0%	9%	35%	55%

20. I comment on student writing so students can improve on the next paper.

	0%	0%	6%	29%	65%

21. Students' writing improves as a result of the feedback I offer.

	0%	5%	30%	52%	14%

22. Students are accustomed to producing multiple drafts of their writing.

	15%	45%	28%	11%	2%

23. I expect my students to write papers using research.

	2%	5%	25%	40%	29%

24. I discuss one or more elements of the writing process with students individually or as a class.

	2%	6%	19%	38%	36%

25. Students focus too much on grammar and mechanics when revising their work.

	20%	43%	28%	8%	2%

26. Students focus too much on logic and structure when revising their work.

	20%	50%	30%	0%	0%

27. My writing assignments prove challenging for students.

	0%	2%	21%	60%	17%

28. My students are well prepared for challenging writing assignments at the start of the course.

	34%	45%	18%	3%	0%

29. My students are well prepared for challenging writing assignments at the end of the course.

	3%	19%	47%	25%	6%

30. I require that my students write in-class essays rather than writing done outside of class.

	23%	37%	24%	15%	2%

31. I require students to respond to objective questions on exams rather than short answer or essay questions.

	19%	24%	27%	19%	11%

WORKS CITED

"About Bristol Community College." Bristol Community College, http://www.bristolcc.edu, accessed 29 February 2008.

Anson, Chris M. "Response Styles and Ways of Knowing." *Writing and Response: Theory, Practice, and Research*. Ed. Chris M. Anson. Urbana, IL: NCTE, 1989. 332–66.

Armstrong, Cheryl. "Reader-Based and Writer-Based Perspectives in Composition Instruction." *Rhetoric Review* 5, no. 1 (1986): 84–89.

Bailey, Thomas, and Timothy Leinbach Davis Jenkins. *Community College Low-Income and Minority Student Completion Study: Descriptive Statistics from the 1992 High School Cohort*. New York: Columbia University, Teachers College, Community College Research Center, 2005.

Bartholomae, David, and Anthony Petrosky. *Ways of Reading: An Anthology for Writers*. 8th ed. New York: Bedford/St. Martin's, 2008.

Beach, Richard. "Self-Evaluation Strategies of Extensive Revisers and Non-Revisers." *College Composition and Communication* 27 (May 1976): 160–64.

Britton, James, Tony Burgess, Nancy Martin, Alex McLeod, and Harold Rosen. *The Development of Writing Abilities (11–18)*. London: Macmillan Education, 1975.

Broad, Bob. *What We Really Value: Beyond Rubrics in Teaching and Assessing Writing*. Logan: Utah State UP, 2003.

Carroll, Lee Ann. *Rehearsing New Roles; How College Students Develop as Writers*. Carbondale: SIUP, 2002.

Carter, Michael. "Ways of Knowing, Doing, and Writing in the Disciplines." *College Composition and Communication* 58 (2007): 385–418.

Chiseri-Strater, Elizabeth. "Turning In upon Ourselves: Positionality, Subjectivity, In Case Study and Ethnographic Research." In *Ethics and Representation in Qualitative Studies of Literacy*. Ed. Peter Mortensen and Gesa E. Kirsch. Urbana, IL: NCTE, 1996. 115–33.

Community College Survey of Student Engagement (CCSSE). "Committing to Student Engagement: Reflecting on CCSSE's First Five Years, 2007 Findings." http://www.ccsse.org/publications/2007NatlRpt-final.pdf, accessed 3 March 2008.

Dougherty, Kevin J. *The Contradictory College: The Conflicting Origins, Impacts, and Futures of the Community College*. Albany: State U of NY, 2001.

Donoghue, Frank. *The Last Professors*. New York: Fordham UP, 2008.

Durst, Russel K. *Collision Course: Conflict, Negotiation, and Learning in College Composition.* Urbana, IL.: NCTE, 1999.

Emig, Janet. *The Composing Processes of Twelfth Graders.* Urbana: NCTE, 1971.

"Employment Status of Community College by Enrollment Status: 1995–1996." American Association of Community Colleges, http://www.aacc.nche.edu/pdf/AboutCC_Fulltime.pdf, accessed 3 July 2008.

"Faculty Degree Attainment." CC Stats. American Association of Community Colleges, http:// www2.aacc.nche.edu/research/index_faculty.htm, accessed 31 July 2008.

Flower, Linda. "Writer-Based Prose: A Cognitive Basis for Problems in Writing." *College English* 41, no. 1 (1979): 19–37.

Flower, Linda S., John R. Hayes, Linda Carey, Karen Schriver, and James Stratman. "Detection, Diagnosis, and the Strategies of Revision." *College Composition and Communication* 37 (February 1986): 16–55.

Grubb, W. Norton, and associates. *Honored but Invisible: An Inside Look at Teaching in Community Colleges.* New York: Routledge, 1999.

Haswell, Richard. "The Complexities of Responding to Student Writing; or, Looking for Shortcuts via the Road of Excess." *Across the Disciplines: Interdisciplinary Perspectives on Language, Learning, and Academic Writing* 3 (9 Nov. 2006): 1–30. http://wac.colostate.edu/atd/articles/haswell2006.cfm, accessed 9 February 2008.

———. *Gaining Ground in College Writing: Tales of Development in College Writing.* Dallas: SMUP, 1991.

Heath, Shirley Brice. *Ways with Words: Language, Life, and Work in Communities and Classrooms.* New York: Cambridge UP, 1983.

Herrington, Anne J., and Marcia Curtis. *Persons in Process: Four Stories of Writing and Personal Development in College.* Urbana, IL: NCTE, 2000.

Hillocks, Jr.,QQQ George. *Teaching Writing as a Reflective Practice.* New York: Teachers College, 1995.

"History of BCC." Bristol Community College, http://www.bristolcc.edu, accessed 29 February 2008.

Huot, Brian. *(Re)Articulating Writing Assessment for Teaching and Learning.* Logan: Utah State UP, 2002.

Kegan, Robert. *In Over our Heads: The Mental Demands of Modern Life.* Cambridge: Harvard UP, 1994.

Kitzhaber, Albert R. *Themes, Theories and Therapy: The Teaching of Writing in College.* New York: McGraw Hill, 1963.

Knoblauch, C. H., and Lil Brannon. *Rhetorical Traditions and the Teaching of Writing.* Upper Montclair, NJ: Boynton/Cook, 1984.

Labov, William. *The Study of Nonstandard English*. Urbana, IL.: NCTE, 1970.

Levin, Henry M., and Juan Carlos Calcagno. "Remediation in the Community College." *Community College Review* 35, no. 3 (2008): 181–207. Academic Search Premier. Bristol Community College Lib. Fall River, MA. Accessed 4 March 2008.

Light, Richard. *Making the Most of College: Students Speak Their Minds*. Cambridge: Harvard UP, 2001.

Lunsford, Andrea. "The Content of Basic Writers' Essays." *College Composition and Communication* 31 (October 1980): 278–90.

Massachusetts Community College Council (MCCC). "Research Vital to MCCC Mission." *MCCC News* 6, no. 2 (February 2008): 4.

"NEASC Self-Study 2004." Bristol Community College: Prepared for the Commission on Institutions of Higher Education New England Association of Schools and Colleges. January 2004.

Roethke, Theodore. *The Collected Poems*. New York: Anchor, 1974.

Rose, Mike. *Lives on the Boundary*. New York: Penguin, 1989.

———. *Writer's Block: The Cognitive Dimension*. Carbondale: SIUP, 1984.

Russell, David. *Writing in the Academic Disciplines: A Curricular History*. 2nd ed. Carbondale: SIUP, 2002.

Schön, Donald. *The Reflective Practitioner: How Professionals Think in Action*. New York: Basic Books, 1983.

Shaughnessy, Mina. *Errors and Expectations: A Guide for the Teacher of Basic Writing*. New York: Oxford UP, 1977.

Shulman, Lee. *Teaching as Community Property: Essays on Higher Education*. San Francisco: Jossey-Bass, 2004.

Smitherman, Geneva. *Talkin' and Testifyin'*. Boston: Houghton, Mifflin, 1977.

Sommers, Nancy. "Revision Strategies of Student Writers and Experienced Writers." *Composition and Communication* 31 (December 1980): 378–88.

Sommers, Nancy, and Laura Saltz. "The Novice as Expert: Writing the Freshman Year." *Composition and Communication* 56 (September 2004): 124–49.

"Starting Right: A First Look at Engaging Entering Students." Community College Survey of Student Engagement and the Carnegie Foundation for the Advancement of Teaching, http://www.ccsse.org/sense/SENSE_report07-FINAL.pdf, accessed 3 July 2007.

Sternglass, Marilyn. *Time to Know Them: A Longitudinal Study of Writing and Learning at the College Level*. Mahwah, NJ: Lawrence Erlbaum, 1997.

Thaiss, Chris, and Terry Myers Zawacki. *Engaged Writers and Dynamic Disciplines: Research on the Academic Writing Life.* Portsmouth, NH: Boynton/Cook, 2006.

Tinberg, Howard, Donna Killian Duffy, and Jack Mino. "The Scholarship of Teaching and Learning at the Two-Year College: Promise and Peril." *Change.* (July/August 2007): 26–33.

Tingle, Nick. *Self Development and College Writing.* Carbondale: SIUP, 2004.

TYCA (Two-Year College English Association). "Tuition." *TYCA Two-Year College Facts and Data Report,* http://www.ntce.org/groups/tyca/featuredinfo/122335.htm, accessed 27 February 2008.

———. "Two-Year College Faculty Profile: Employment Status, Gender, Ethnicity." *TYCA Two-Year College Facts and Data Report,* http://www.ntce.org/groups/tyca/featuredinfo/122335.htm, accessed 27 February 2008.

———. "Two-Year College Student Body Profile." *TYCA Two-Year College Facts and Data Report,* http://www.ntce.org/groups/tyca/featuredinfo/122335.htm, accessed 27 February 2008.

———. "Two-Year/Four-Year Full-Time/Part-Time Tenure Status" *TYCA Two-Year College Facts and Data Report,* http://www.ntce.org/groups/tyca/featuredinfo/122335.htm, accessed 28 February 2008.

Walvoord, Barbara E., and Lucille McCarthy. *Thinking and Writing in College: A Naturalistic Study of Students in Four Disciplines.* Urbana, IL: NCTE, 1990.

Welch, Nancy. *Getting Restless: Rethinking Writing and Revision.* Portsmouth, NH: Boynton/Cook, 1997.

INDEX

active learners, fostering, 124–25
analytical skills of students, 2
Andrew (student), 106–14; argumentative essay, 112–13; background, 106–7; biographical sketch, 108–9; confidence as writer, 107; film review, 112–14; and instructor feedback, 110; research paper, 108–9; writing process, 109–10
assignments. *See* writing assignments

Bartholomae, David, 7
Basic Writing courses, 13, 19, 99
Ben (student), 82–90; background, 82–83; classification paper, 87–88; confidence of, 90; definition essay, 88–89; descriptive/narrative essay, 85–87; high school experience, 83; marketing plan, 84; resume for accounting class, 84–85
Bristol Community College, 37–38
Britton, James, 15

career-oriented writing, 132
Carroll, Lee Ann, 18
categorical thinking, 67–68
certificate programs, 7
College Writing course: and commitment to student writing, 128; Kim (student) and, 71, 73; Nicole (student) and, 93–98; preparedness for, 60
communication, writing assignments in, 116
community college faculty, 8, 36–38. *See also* faculty *entries*

community colleges: culture of, and teaching approaches, 7; mission of, 6, 46; remediation crisis at, 38; represented in student survey of attitudes, 59
community college students, 4, 20, 57–58. *See also* student *entries*
Community College Survey of Student Engagement (CCSSE), 37
composition, in the 1980s, 15–16
conferences with students, one-on-one, 126
confidence in writing abilities: Andrew (student), 107–8; Ben (student), 90; of cohort compared to other students surveyed, 59–60; drafts and, 125; Kim (student), 70–72, 82
consciousness, Kegan's levels of, 68
constructivist pedagogical approach, 37
cross-categorical knowing, 67–69, 98
cultural studies approach, 13
culture shock, 6

developmental approach to teaching, 125, 130
disconnects between instructor and student, 66
drafts, faculty response to, 11–12, 55, 129–30. *See also* revisions
durable category, 70

education, ownership of, 72
elitism, scholarly discussion and perception of, 8

153

CCCC STUDIES IN WRITING & RHETORIC

Edited by Joseph Harris, Duke University

The aim of the CCCC Studies in Writing & Rhetoric (SWR) series is to influence how writing gets taught at the college level. The methods of studies vary from the critical to historical to linguistic to ethnographic, and their authors draw on work in various fields that inform composition—including rhetoric, communication, education, discourse analysis, psychology, cultural studies, and literature. Their focuses are similarly diverse—ranging from individual writers and teachers, to classrooms and communities and curricula, to analyses of the social, political, and material contexts of writing and its teaching. Still, all SWR volumes try in some way to inform the practice of writing students, teachers, or administrators. Their approach is synthetic, their style concise and pointed. Complete manuscripts run from 40,000 to 50,000 words, or about 150 to 200 pages. Authors should imagine their work in the hands of writing teachers as well as on library shelves.

SWR was one of the first scholarly book series to focus on the teaching of writing. It was established in 1980 by the Conference on College Composition and Communication (CCCC) to promote research in the emerging field of writing studies. Since its inception, the series has been copublished by Southern Illinois University Press. As the field has grown, the research sponsored by SWR has continued to articulate the commitment of CCCC to supporting the work of writing teachers as reflective practitioners and intellectuals. For a list of previous SWR books, see the SWR link on the SIU Press Web site at www.siu.edu/~siupress.

We are eager to identify influential work in writing and rhetoric as it emerges. We thus ask authors to send us project proposals that clearly situate their work in the field and show how they aim to redirect our ongoing conversations about writing and its teaching. Proposals should include an overview of the project, a brief annotated table of contents, and a sample chapter. They should not exceed 10,000 words.

To submit a proposal or to contact the series editor, please go to http://uwp.aas.duke.edu/cccc/swr/.

*Revisionary Rhetoric, Feminist
Pedagogy, and Multigenre Texts*
Julie Jung

*Women Writing the Academy:
Audience, Authority, and
Transformation*
Gesa E. Kirsch

Invention as a Social Act
Karen Burke LeFevre

*A New Perspective on Cohesion in
Expository Paragraphs*
Robin Bell Markels

*Response to Reform:
Composition and the
Professionalization of Teaching*
Margaret J. Marshall

*Before Shaughnessy: Basic Writing at
Yale and Harvard, 1920–1960*
Kelly Ritter

*Gender Influences: Reading
Student Texts*
Donnalee Rubin

*The Young Composers:
Composition's Beginnings in
Nineteenth-Century Schools*
Lucille M. Schultz

Multiliteracies for a Digital Age
Stuart A. Selber

*Technology and Literacy in
the Twenty-First Century: The
Importance of Paying Attention*
Cynthia L. Selfe

*Language Diversity in the Classroom:
From Intention to Practice*
Edited by Geneva Smitherman and
Victor Villanueva

*Whistlin' and Crowin' Women
of Appalachia: Literacy Practices
since College*
Katherine Kelleher Sohn

*Across Property Lines: Textual
Ownership in Writing Groups*
Candace Spigelman

*Personally Speaking: Experience as
Evidence in Academic Discourse*
Candace Spigelman

Self-Development and College Writing
Nick Tingle

*Mutuality in the Rhetoric and
Composition Classroom*
David L. Wallace and
Helen Rothschild Ewald

*A Taste for Language: Literacy,
Class, and English Studies*
James Ray Watkins

Evaluating College Writing Programs
Stephen P. Witte and Lester Faigley

*Minor Re/Visions: Asian American
Literacy Narratives as a Rhetoric
of Citizenship*
Morris Young

Howard Tinberg, professor of English at Bristol Community College, Massachusetts, is the author of *Border Talk: Writing and Knowing in the Two-Year College*, *Writing with Consequence: What Writing Does in the Disciplines;* and coeditor (with Pat Sullivan) of *What Is "College-Level" Writing?*

Jean-Paul Nadeau, coauthor of *Foundations for Learning*, is an assistant professor of English at Bristol Community College.